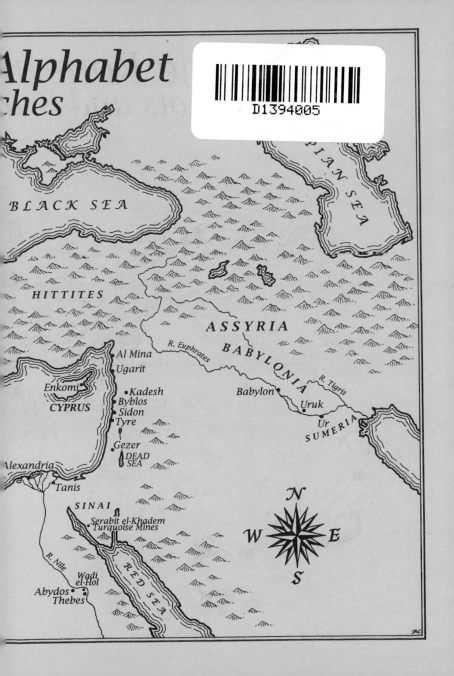

Alphabet
ches

D1394005

BLACK SEA

CASPIAN SEA

HITTITES

ASSYRIA

BABYLONIA

R. Euphrates

R. Tigris

Al Mina
Ugarit
Enkomi
CYPRUS
Kadesh
Byblos
Babylon
Sidon
Tyre
Uruk
Gezer
Ur
DEAD SEA
SUMERIA

Alexandria

Tanis

SINAI
Serabit el-Khadem
Turquoise Mines

N
W   E
S

R. Nile
Wadi el-Hol
Abydos
Thebes

RED SEA

ALPHA BETA

ALPHA BETA

HOW OUR ALPHABET CHANGED

THE WESTERN WORLD

JOHN MAN

HEADLINE

First published in 2000
by HEADLINE BOOK PUBLISHING

10 9 8 7 6 5 4 3 2 1

British Library Cataloguing in Publication Data
A Catalogue record of this book
is available from the British Library.

ISBN 0 7472 7136 4

Typeset by
Letterpart Limited, Reigate, Surrey

Printed and bound in Great Britain by
Clays Ltd, St Ives plc

HEADLINE BOOK PUBLISHING
A division of Hodder Headline
338 Euston Road
London NW1 3BH

www.headline.co.uk
www.hodderheadline.com

For Timberlake and Dushka

CONTENTS

FOREWORD

This book is about one of humanity's greatest ideas – the idea of alphabet – and its most widespread form: the system of letters you are now reading. Three features of the idea stand out: its uniqueness, its simplicity and its adaptability. From the alphabet's earliest manifestation 4000 years ago, all other alphabets take their cue; and all reflect the idea's underlying simplicity.

This is not the simplicity of perfect design. The strength of the alphabet as an idea lies in its practical imperfection. Though it fits no language to perfection, it can, with some pushing and shoving, be adapted to all languages. Like our own big-brained species, which can be outrun, outflown and outswum, but not outthought, by other species, the alphabet is a generalist. In software terms, its success lies in its 'fuzziness'. But where did this idea of alphabet spring from? How and where did it spread as it matured into the Roman-letter system that is now the world's most familiar script? How did we discover the answer to these questions?

It is a good time to examine such things, because the roots of the alphabet are still emerging. It seems increasingly certain that this revolutionary, one-off concept arose in Egypt, about 2000 BC. These discoveries will remain controversial until more evidence is found, interpreted and accepted, but one thing you can bet on: as archaeology becomes ever more effective, astonishing advances are still to be made. One day, perhaps, some cache of scrolls or inscriptions will reveal the genii – perhaps even the individual genius – who mined the first treasure-trove of letters from Egyptian hieroglyphs.

I focus on the idea and its transmission from culture to culture, from Egypt, to Rome, to us. It seems to me that I had little option in this choice of theme, for otherwise there would be no end. A full history of the alphabet would be a library, with specialist sections on scores of alphabetical systems and their cultures, on the impact of literacy down the centuries, on the psychology of reading, the techniques of writing, the strange worlds of magi who turned the ABC into 'abracadabra'. Each letter has its own history. There is little in this book about technical advances or grand historical processes – the papyrus trade, printing, imperialism, the Internet. These are the tides that carry the western alphabet across the world, but they have little impact on the

Roman alphabetical code, let alone the underlying idea that unites alphabetical scripts from Abaza to Zulu – that all human speech can be symbolized by two or three dozen meaningless marks.

INTRODUCTION: OF GIANTS AND GENIUS

A s a child, I went to an old-fashioned little boarding school in Hastings where the headmaster was a one-eyed giant. He was 6' 4" and weighed 280 pounds and he had a glass eye. I have no idea how he lost the real one. The glass eye had the disconcerting habit of oozing liquid, so that in mid-tirade, on the verge of applying the cane, he would produce a handkerchief and wipe away a crocodile tear. It was rumoured, though I never saw it for myself, that he could take his eye out, polish it and replace it.

So when I first heard of the Cyclops, the one-eyed ogre in the *Odyssey*, I knew exactly what Odysseus was up against. I see myself as an eleven-year-old in grey flannel shorts, tie with horizontal yellow-and-black stripes, knuckles raw with some winter rash, sitting at one of those old wooden desks with a sloping, lift-up top, on which someone has carved his initials, 'CP'. Kennedy's *Latin Primer*, long since turned into *'Eating' Primer* by a schoolboy scribble, lies in front of me, unopened. Mr Marshall is an enlightened teacher and, although this is double Latin, it being Wednesday afternoon, he has chosen, as usual, to abandon Latin for the *Odyssey*. This is not a Greek lesson exactly – the language is only for the scholarship boys – but a reading of the newish translation by E. V. Rieu. Its images, vivid as film, transport me . . .

. . . to the cave where Odysseus and his men have been trapped by the shambling Cyclops. Illustrations show him with a single eye in the middle of his forehead, but I see him as our headmaster, minus his glass eye, dressed in skins instead of his brown pin-striped suit. The Cyclops (meaning 'round-eyed') blocks the cave mouth with a rock that twenty-two four-wheeled wagons could not have carried. He seizes two of the Greeks, dashes their heads against the floor, splatters the rocks with their brains, tears them limb from limb, and crunches them up, ravenous as a lion with a new kill. Odysseus watches, stricken. I had an inkling of how he felt. Once, guilty of talking after lights out, I had stood in line outside the headmaster's study, hearing the six-fold thwacks on friend after friend. I knew the dread of approaching doom. Now here was Homer, showing me what it was like to be cunning, brave and strong enough to save friends from giants. Odysseus offers wine and then, when the Cyclops falls into a drunken stupor, prepares a stave, huge as the mast of a twenty-oared ship, heats it in the fire and, with five of his men, rams it into the Cyclops' single eye. 'I used my weight from above to twist it home, like a man boring a ship's timber with a drill . . . In much the same way we handled our pole with its red-hot point and twisted it in his eye till the blood boiled around the burning wood. The fiery smoke of the blazing eyeball singed his lids and brow all round, and the very roots of his eye crackled in the heat. I was reminded of the loud hiss that comes from a great axe or adze when a smith plunges it into cold water – to temper it and give strength to the iron. That is how the Cyclops eye hissed around that olive stake.' I glance round, exchange grimaces, and feel the glow of a shared response. Yes, we all love every gory, vengeful detail.

From those vivid readings, from the fact that Mr Marshall made time for them, from their emotional impact, I received a clear message: this story – speaking so directly from so remote a time – mattered. Not that I knew why. I had no idea that I was being given an introduction to the roots of a culture in which my own was rooted. In the introduction to his own translation, T. E. Lawrence, a classical scholar as well as co-liberator of Arabia, called the *Odyssey* 'the oldest book worth reading for its story and the first novel of Europe'. It was the start of a line leading another three centuries right to the burst of creative energy that made the Athens of the fifth century BC a cornucopia of philosophy, science and literature, pouring out creations whose effects rippled down the centuries and across continents.

The consequences are all around. The fields of study founded by the Greeks or coined from Greek words run from astronomy and biology all the way through the alphabet to xylography and zoology. When looking for their roots, European cultures (except perhaps the Basques) quickly dig up Greeks. So do most white – or even Latino – Americans, Australians and other scattered ex-European lineages. So, in lesser ways, do Muslims, because their scholars were translating Aristotle into Arabic when Europe was still in its post-Roman limbo. To Afghans and Uzbeks, Alexander the Great is a vivid folk memory. Anyone learning a European language or studying the history of anywhere from the Hebrides to the Hindu Kush will come across the Greeks eventually. In language, the Greeks are with us still, as real and as forgotten as a childhood taste. You could probably write a novel using only ordinary nouns and verbs derived from the Greek, certainly a dissertation, because its root-words so readily form techno-speak, as in: '*Genetics* and *character*: The use of *cybernetics* in *psychological analysis*.' Today's coins have a head on one side and a symbol on the other because that was the way the Greeks did it.

Why this tide of Greekness? Were there special things about ancient Greek genes or society or technology or food or climate, or any combination of these, that created the intellectual bloom? Of the many answers, one intrigues me. It is the suggestion that Homer and his successors had an impact only because their words were recorded in a form that allowed their thoughts to be transferred easily from generation to generation. The Greeks, so this argument runs, would not have been so influential but for the invention that fixed their writings, the invention that they named after its first two signs, alpha and beta – the alphabet.

The alphabet? It is a little hard to know what exactly the 'the' refers to, because there are many so-called alphabets which do not begin with *a* and *b*. Ogham, the Old Irish system, began BLF; Germany's medieval script, Runic, started with six letters after which it is named, the futhark ('th' being a single letter). Ethiopic began h-l. Some early 'alphabets' broke down after the first two letters into abjads or abugidas. But despite the changes, an ideal runs through them all: that the sounds of speech can be captured by a collection of two or three dozen single signs, each of which corresponds to a spoken sound. In fact, as we shall see, this is a vain hope. But the ideal remains, a dream of the perfect written communication. It is this ideal that inspired this book, which examines the emergence of our own alphabet from its Egyptian roots through to the Latinized form which you are reading now. This book takes as its subject the alphabet as a unit, not dealing in depth with the overwhelmingly vast subjects of writing, the technicalities of script or the histories of individual letters.

Many have been convinced that the Greek alphabet was the best of the lot, because (they claim) it was the direct cause of the flowering of Greek genius and all that followed. This suggestion was most forcefully put in the 1970s by the Anglo-American academic, Eric Havelock, the late professor of classics at Yale. The alphabet, he maintained, was one of the great leaps, a stroke of genius which, like the invention of fire or the wheel, ensured that life in the western world would never be the same again.

As a result, he said, the Greeks were able to turn works of recitation into works of literature. The *Odyssey* and the *Iliad*, which would otherwise have been lost, were the first major works captured for posterity, like photographs of birds in flight. Havelock would have told me that it was not merely Homer's genius, or Greek genius, that guaranteed the survival of his works. It was the fact that a scribe, or team of scribes, had been able to fix the stories in a form of writing that no culture had fully exploited before. With this new-fangled intellectual device, the

Greeks could record their own thought processes, become self-aware, refine ideas, exchange them, build upon them, create systems of ethics, philosophy and science, evolve new forms of poetry, pioneer history and biography. In brief, it was the alphabet that allowed the ancient Greeks to lay the foundations of civilized discourse as Europe and its descendant cultures came to know it.

Inventions like this are rare: intellectual tools that are both independent of technology and explosive in impact. Writing itself is an equivalent, perhaps, and the invention of the 'Arabic' numbering system (actually, it was originally Indian), in particular zero, which formed the basis of modern mathematics. Perhaps grand ideas like monotheism and evolution have had a comparable effect. Yet such ideas spring up in many different guises, often in different times and different places, before they are accepted. Writing was invented perhaps four times: in China, Mesopotamia, Egypt and Central America ('perhaps' because there are those who argue that the Egyptians took over the idea, though not the form, from Mesopotamia). The base-ten numbering system also emerged four times independently: in Babylon, China, India and Central America. Monotheism arose independently in the Old and New World (a generalization I can defend, in a small way, by citing a tribe with which I spent some time in 1979–80, the Waorani of the eastern Ecuadorian jungle; they believed in a single god, Waengongi, from long before the arrival of Europeans). And evolution had an evolution of its own from long before it was formalized by Darwin.

But the alphabet, despite its multifarious forms, was a unique idea, arising only once, spreading across cultures and down centuries. There are many other writing systems, but they are all ideographic or syllabic. Other than the unknown scribes who originated the first tentative form of the alphabet around 2000 BC in Egypt, no culture or person ever independently dreamed up the idea. All those hundred or so who have ever used an alphabetical system either distilled it from a previous system, or inherited or adapted an established alphabet, or heard of the idea, and made up their own on that basis. In Havelock's words, it was a uniquely efficient way of recording human speech, and 'once invented, it supplied the complete answer to a problem, and there has never been a need to reinvent it'.

Havelock's claim seems to agree with everyday experience. Our letters are so simple and practical that we give the shapes to babies to play with and turn the sounds into a song with which two-year-olds charm proud parents. The consequences have been fundamental to all the world, directly to those of us who use alphabets, and indirectly to those who don't, because they get the benefits in translation. The effects are part of the extraordinary acceleration in the process by which our biological evolution, pretty much fixed 100,000 years ago, has been overlaid by – even hijacked by – cultural evolution running on time-scales tens, hundreds, thousands of times faster, accelerating us into the unknowable.

Ignoring for a moment regional differences and focusing on leading indicators, cultural evolution forms an ever-steepening graph plotted along major advances; first, the 4000-year climb from literacy towards bookishness, using any material to hand: stone, wood, papyrus, wax, velum. Transmission of information with these cumbersome media was measured in centuries, while the literati in the few literate societies made up only about 1% of the population. With the invention of wood-block printing on paper in China in the eighth century, literacy started to spread, speeding up again with the invention of movable type in China in the mid-eleventh century, and in Europe, with far greater impact, in the fifteenth century. Transmission of information during this millennium took decades. With the growth of industry in the nineteenth century, decades compressed to years, and then, with air travel, to weeks. Now that cultural evolution has become electronic, information flows worldwide in seconds, and illiteracy is a synonym for backwardness.

The coarsest measure of the explosion in literacy and information is to look at the sheer weight of written and published material. In AD 500, Europe was turning out about 200,000 volumes per year, while China had been producing about 800,000 a year for centuries: a million books, say 500 tons of paper. At the turn of the millennium, the world produced some *ten billion* books a year – about 50 million tons of paper, for books alone. Now add in newspapers – 8391 dailies as I write, and rising – and weekly and monthly magazines – 73,000 titles. In all, for communicating, the world produces about 130 million tons of paper a year – 50 pounds per person. In 500 years, when the world's population has risen 13-fold, the literate population has risen 1000-fold, and reading materials over 250,000 times, almost all the increase in this century. Per person, we consume almost 20,000 times as much reading material as our medieval ancestors. Over 60 per cent of the world's total consumption of written material is in alphabets of one kind or another.

In terms of content, of course, almost all of this verbiage dies with its paper, in a day. Most of the rest is dead within a year. But from this physical mulch, and increasingly from its electronic equivalent, springs almost every aspect of the culture of advanced societies, directly or indirectly. This is a change so significant in human society that we should really declare ourselves to be a new sub-species: *homo sapiens literariensis*.

About 80 million tons of paper printed with alphabets of various sorts is a phenomenon that demands an explanation independent of its underlying cultural mutation, writing. The trail quickly leads back to the Greeks, and to a number of issues raised by Havelock's thesis.

Was the explosion of alphabet-based literacy really the key to Greek genius? Havelock's grand claims, advanced in several different forms over many years, caused increasingly violent reactions in the halls of Academe. First, some of his contemporary classicists objected. Havelock was an acerbic, left-wing Yorkshireman, who had made it across the Atlantic and into the portals of the Ivy League, and there were those who did not like to be told that the true explanation of Greek genius lay in something as mundane as two dozen simple signs.

Later, after Havelock's death in 1985, a different set of objections emerged from among those who championed other ancient cultures. If the alphabet was uniquely efficient, why has the Chinese writing system endured so long? Are we to conclude that Chinese culture is 'inferior' because it has not adopted a system that is supposedly superior? Were we to thank only the Greeks for founding western culture, forgetting predecessors like the Egyptians and Assyrians, whose cultures endured almost ten times as long? And the Hebrews, whose first drafts of their holy book almost certainly predate Homer? Had there not been great cities, great cultures, great thinkers, philosophers and poets before? If the Greeks are to be seen as paragons of intellectual achievement, does this not denigrate their predecessors? This last point was made explicit by Havelock when he wrote disparagingly of works recorded in more ancient writing systems. Setting Homer against the 'so-called literatures of the ancient Near East', he concluded: 'The basic complexity of human experience is not there.'

This seems a little harsh, because ancient Greece was not the one and only fount. The ancient Greeks did not *invent* the alphabet. It was in the air, so to speak, for over a thousand years before the Greeks got hold of it. Possibly nothing of their oral genius would have been preserved but for a piece of astonishing good fortune. They just happened to live near one of the cultures that had stumbled on the alphabet, and they just happened to be at a crucial stage in social evolution that made them open to its adoption. Only by looking further back can we understand where and why the alphabet arose, why it appealed to some and not to others, and what role the Greeks performed in accepting, adapting and transmitting it to us.

1

THE TROUBLE
WITH PICTURES

I n the fifteenth century, when a few philosophers began to wonder about the mysteries left by ancient peoples in the Nile valley, the idea arose that the pictures on Egyptian tombs were the purest form of communication. It was an odd notion, given that no one had a clue what they meant, but it was based on what classical authors had written centuries before, and that had the smack of authority. So it was assumed that in these pictures, Nature herself had been captured in a mystic code, and would address the elevated soul in her own pure tones, without the necessity for anything as base as script which, like language, reflected mere babble, in its biblical sense – the confusion imposed by God on mankind by the destruction of the

Tower of Babel. There were, of course, those who claimed to be on suitably intimate terms with Nature. A sixteenth-century Jesuit antiquarian, Athanasius Kircher, set about interpreting hieroglyphic, starting with an obelisk now standing in Rome's Piazza Minerva. One little sequence of signs merely records the name of a sixth-century BC ruler: 'King Apries'. This is Kircher's confident interpretation: 'The protection of Osiris against the violence of Typho must be elicited according to the proper rites and ceremonies by sacrifices and by appeal to the tutelary Genii of the triple world, in order to ensure the enjoyment of the prosperity customarily given by the Nile against the violence of the enemy Typho.'

It was all nonsense. Hieroglyphs are not 'pictures'. They are signs, and syllables, and letters, and experts now read some of them almost as easily as they read their own script. The magic, in its eighteenth-century mystical sense, has gone.

An underlying magic remains, of course: that of literacy itself. It is an astonishing thing that human beings should be able to see marks on a surface and hear them talk of realities visible and invisible. But if Nature is to be understood through writing, she has to be pinned down, summarized, abstracted and recorded by one intelligence in a form understandable by another. For that, the two must share the same, or overlapping, assumptions. Without those links, pictures – whether cave paintings or computer-screen icons – can never be enough to transfer meaning from mind to mind. No one unversed in computers would know what the hieroglyphs along the top of a screen are for. Even the simplest ones, like the cut-and-paste symbols, refer to a technique few have ever used. Click-and-drag, yes; tear-and-staple, perhaps; but cut-and-paste? Not these days. It works, of course, because we all played at cutting and pasting as children and because PC-users learn a shared hyper-language, computerese. But as the cultural links stretch, understanding becomes obscured. Does the image of a figure in a skirt say 'female toilet' to a kilt-wearing Scot as surely as it does to trousered Sassenachs? A hard-hat symbol means 'wear hardhats (and if you don't have one get one)', but a wheelchair symbol does not mean 'sit in a wheelchair (and if you don't have one, get one)'. Ambiguities can never be ironed out with pictures alone, because the human brain is not set up to process them as it processes language. The 2000 or so separate images that can be stored by the average brain, with effort, are as nothing compared to the 50,000 words which most literate people can muster in most languages with ease. It is an enduring dream, this mystical belief that somehow mind can read mind through pure imagery, but there is no transcendental written language, and can never be one. Here are three true stories which show the inadequacy of pictures, and the necessity of script.

South from Iraklion on Crete's northern coast, the road leads through vineyards, into mountains, up to the Askyphos Pass. Beyond a rise of seared grass and gnarled trees, a glorious view unfolds: a quilt of olive groves, orchards and wheat fields, running away to distant hills. This is the plain of Mesara, a rich area for 4000 years. As Bronze Age tombs reveal, the well-to-do, after lives spent trading oil, cereals, wine and figs, were buried swathed in rings, necklaces and diadems, and surrounded with obsidian, gold, silver, copper, tin and elephant ivory. By 1700 BC, the culture named after King Minos controlled all Crete. Palaces – Knossos, Malia, Zakros – dominated these plains and their ports. Ahead, pale in the distance, the land rises to a low plateau, and ruins. There, another of the great Minoan palaces once stood: Phaistos.

Phaistos, or 'Festos' in its more recent transliteration, is the site of one of the world's most intriguing and baffling finds, made by an Italian archaeologist, Louis Pernier, a century ago. This was a time of high emotion, both political and academic. Crete was in turmoil, emerging bloodily from Turkish rule, while archaeologists sought primacy for themselves and their countries by wringing fact from myths and buried rubble. On the Turkish and Greek mainlands, Heinrich Schliemann had uncovered the ruins of Troy and the treasures of Mycenaean kings, and planned to match these achievements in Crete. But in the face of Greek violence and Turkish oppression, Schliemann pulled out, leaving the ground to the Englishman, Arthur Evans. He began digging in Knossos in early 1900, revealing the outlines of the entirely unknown culture he named 'Minoan' after its greatest king, Minos. Italian archaeologists wanted matching glory. Pernier's boss, Federico Halbherr, who had already made stupendous finds on the plain of Mesara, ordered Pernier to look beyond, to Phaistos. It was a promising site, for it was listed by Homer among the homes of those who mustered before the siege of Troy.

In the spring of 1900, Pernier and his team, based in a nearby monastery, sunk the first trenches across the ruins. Over the next few years, the outlines of a great palace of a hundred rooms emerged. Off to one side, gypsum paving led to the remains of eight little storerooms. On the afternoon of 3 July 1908, some of Pernier's team scratching away at earth, ash, charcoal and some bits of pottery in the eighth storeroom, came across a disc of baked clay about 16 cm (6 inches) across. On each side was a spiral of 241 little pictures (242 if you include one that seems to have been erased). It was writing, of an unknown kind.

Minoan officials long kept their accounts in writing, incising symbols on clay. Originally this had been simple picture-writing, so-called Cretan hieroglyphic. Later, by 1700 BC, Cretans had devised a second script now known as 'Linear A', which is still undeciphered. Later still, after

21

the fall of the Minoans, Greek colonists used a third script, 'Linear B'. But the Phaistos Disc was written in none of these, nor in any other known script.

Pottery found nearby and the architectural style of the storeroom both suggested the disc was squirreled away around 1700 BC. This is not a date to swear by, for other, later pottery was found in the same little room, and besides the disc could have been moved during excavation. Pernier's workmen made their find in the morning; Pernier turned up in the late afternoon, impeccably dressed, to be shown the day's work; so it could be that the disc was made later, but somehow strayed into earlier shards. If it was made around 1700 BC, the date is of some significance for Minoan studies, for about this time Minoan palaces went up in smoke, probably as the result of an earthquake, followed by looting. From this catastrophe the Minoans recovered, rebuilding anew on the foundations of the old. In Phaistos, the palace was restored, but no one bothered with the little storeroom and its enigmatic contents. It lay hidden or forgotten, until Pernier unearthed it.

Since then, scholars and lay people have puzzled over the disc, now in the Iraklion Museum, and over its copies, and over enlarged photographs, wringing information from it. The most astonishing thing about the disc is that the crisp little signs are not drawn on the clay. They are carefully printed, by well-made, hard stamps. This makes the disc the first known example of printing.

Clearly, it was not a one-off. The stamps would have been used to print other clay tablets. What were the stamps made of? Wood? No: the images are too hard-edged. Even if some superb carver had made the blocks, they would have worn quickly with use. It is hard to imagine wood-carvers making set after set. The blocks would have been made of metal. And since bronze and iron are coarse in detail, the best material for making such stamps was gold, cast in clay moulds.

Detective work has revealed a few other details. From its irregularity, the disc was hand-made, not set in a mould. Many (some say all) of the 45 individual pictures can be identified – a skirted walker caught in mid-stride, a head with Mohican-style haircut or headdress, a knobbly club, a captive, a child, a woman with wild hair and dangling breasts. They divide into groups, which could be words or phrases. The stylus marks show that the spiral was drawn from the rim inwards, in sections, and that the signs were imprinted as the spiral was drawn. So the script reads anti-clockwise, from rim to centre. One side is stamped more gently, presumably in order not to flatten out the first set of impressions on the obverse.

If it was not Cretan, where did it come from? The eastern Mediterranean in the middle of the second millennium BC was a mix of cultures. Greek culture was in its infancy, but the Egyptians had over a thousand years of development behind them. The Hittites dominated central Turkey, the Assyrians ruled Mesopotamia, the Phoenicians were reaching out from their eastern Mediterranean homeland. All were linked by trade across the Himalayas to a civilization in the Indus Valley. All traded through intermediaries with China. All had their own writing systems. And none of them looked anything like that on the Phaistos Disc. Some culture, probably in the eastern Mediterranean, probably around 2000 BC, found it worthwhile to devise these signs to represent their language.

The signs were probably syllables – because every other local culture wrote in syllables – but possibly individual words, like Chinese, possibly a combination of the two. Some wealthy group then commissioned artisans to make golden stamps, which were used to print messages on clay – an operation that would surely have been done many times, using the same or similar clay moulds, perhaps over many generations. A baked disc makes a handy shape to record signs of this size. There must at one time have been hundreds, thousands, perhaps tens of thousands of such discs scattered across the eastern Mediterranean.

If others survive in some buried archive, a new discovery may one day make all clear. At present, speculation is all we have, in plenty. If the early clay tablets of Sumeria are anything to go by, this could have been an inventory, perhaps that of a cargo ship. But when almost all is guesswork, there is much leeway for eccentricity. A quick search of the Net reveals people convinced the disc is a magical text ('possibly a curse'), a geometrical theorem, a calendar, a Bronze Age computer. Here's someone certain that it records an expedition of mountain people seeking flat land for settlement. Someone else, with messianic self-assurance, states that the disc records the beliefs and practices of the Osiris cult, whose adepts communicated with the stars 'and beyond through interdimensional travel'. You want proof? In the signs, you can make join-the-dot outlines both of the Great Pyramid and the constellation Argo, which means there is a 'star portal' in Argo. Obviously, the disc is a key to the use of 'portal geometry' and the salvation of the soul of the world.

The sad truth is that so little can be gleaned from the disc that it acts as a sort of ink-blot which can be made to mean almost anything you want it to mean. There is not much hope of deriving anything more. It takes many more symbols than this, and some link with a known language, to decipher an unknown script. Unless some bilingual key is found, the disc's language, script and information content will remain for ever enigmatic.

In late 1971, two Pioneer probes were about to be launched on a planetary tour that would eventually take them out of the solar system. Two science writers, Eric Burgess and Richard Hoagland, were shown Pioneer 10 by NASA, and had an idea: 'We decided in a split second

that very afternoon that Pioneer should – must somehow – carry into Infinity a literal "Message from Mankind." '
They put the idea to the astronomer Carl Sagan. Sagan and his wife, Linda Salzmann, were given a few days to devise something suitable.

The aliens would, perhaps, not be sensitive to light in the visible spectrum. But, in the same way that we have discovered how to use X-rays and infrared radiation, these aliens would by definition be advanced enough to retrieve a probe and study its little plaque. They would wish to know the origin of the strange artefact. Would it be possible to communicate this information in a form so pure that it would be independent not simply of language and script, not simply of human culture, but of human intelligence? Was there a way for intelligence to speak to intelligence in written form? Sagan suggested that there was, if the message were engraved on a plaque in a language that is woven into the fabric of the universe. This, he argued, would provide the link with any culture advanced enough to find the Pioneers (for the same plaque was also attached to Pioneer 11, which was also due to leave our solar system).

The plaque uses an atom of the universe's most common element, hydrogen, to provide two units. Its wavelength (21 cm) gives a unit of distance, its frequency (1420 megaHertz, or 1420 million cycles per second) a unit of time. Using just the two on-off symbols of binary code, these units can spell out numbers of any size. Sagan decided to specify the probe's origin. Since our Sun has no special traits to mark it out from a billion others, Sagan focused on stellar rarities known as pulsars, super-dense stars that spin at astonishing rates, averaging about twice per second (with the fastest known pulsar spinning 625 times a second). At each revolution, the star emits a powerful radio pulse. Each pulsar is unique, with its own spin-time that is accurate to one part in 100 million, probably for hundreds of millions of years. Sagan chose fourteen 'local' pulsars and created a star-burst pattern that gave a rough indication of their direction and distance as seen from the centre of the Galaxy. Their frequencies in hydrogen-atom units he labelled in binary. Scientifically advanced aliens would, in theory, know about hydrogen atoms and pulsars, and thus be able to pinpoint the region from which the probes came. Other sections of the plaque sketched our solar system, whose collection of nine planets must surely be unique in this corner of the galaxy. A line connects a Pioneer icon to the third planet.

Sagan also included two odd-shaped patterns, which we see as a man and a woman, both naked. However different the aliens might be, they might perhaps deduce from the very oddity of the patterns that they represent biological objects, even if the extrusions and dangly bits remain inexplicable. A drawing of Pioneer provides a scale.

But here we reach the limits. Information about the universe, coded mathematically, is all very well. Sagan's plaque, like computer icons, may speak in a hyper-language provided by the universe. Athanasius Kircher might have considered himself vindicated: you see, Nature does speak! It certainly *looks* like communication. We shall never know. It will take Pioneer 10 65,000 years just to get out of the Sun's gravitational reach, and some 100,000 years to pass the nearest star, assuming it's heading in that direction. The chances of it ever being found before it is shattered or eroded away by space debris is remote. In fact, more cynical minds point out that the intelligences to whom Sagan directed his message were right here on earth: members of Congress who provided the funding for further space projects, like the Search for Extraterrestrial Intelligence, a line of research close to Sagan's heart, and the general public who, as a result of the publicity generated, would bring pressure to loosen purse-strings. Whatever appeals it may have for aliens, the plaque certainly appeals to those who still hold to the dream of perfect and pure communication.

Despite its complexity, the plaque contains not a shred of human information, other than the shape and size of its two puzzling exemplars, because to convey any more information about us demands language, and language cannot leap the gulf to the stars.

Or even leap cultures.

In the early 1980s the US Nuclear Regulatory

Commission, part of the Department of Energy, was wrestling with the problem of nuclear waste. The government was considering a number of short-term solutions, which included burying the waste hundreds of metres deep in remote desert areas. But this stuff would still be radioactive in 10,000 years. The members of the commission wanted to cover every contingency. Who could guess what the world would be like then? Perhaps it would be an age of technological wizardry, which had long since learned to de-activate uranium. Then again, perhaps not. In a thousand years, let alone ten, cultures fall, languages vanish and barbarians arise. Perhaps the world would have poisoned itself in an orgy of industrial development. So the commissioners assumed the worst – global warming, rising seas, changing ecologies, the usual scenarios of self-induced global catastrophe.

Imagine that survivors are starting afresh. The world is much changed. Grasslands are deserts, former deserts bloom, skyscrapers are mere stumps. Our descendants gaze on ruined cities like Celts who see nothing but ghosts among the fallen stones of Londinium. They settle in the depths of what had once been Arizona and New Mexico. All is sweet forest. Several areas seem particularly attractive, because they lack trees already. The grassland looks ideal for domestic animals, and as if by a miracle there are no natural rivals, no wild grazers and browsers. The reason there are no trees and wild animals, of course, is that radiation is leaking up from below.

But there is a peculiar object that gives this little group pause. It is a monolith, like the one in the film *2001: A Space Odyssey*, shall we say. It was built to last, and it has done so as well as the pyramids (which still endure, poking up through the floods of a vastly extended Mediterranean). On it are sets of pictures. Their purpose mirrors the worst and the best of a vanished civilization. Beneath the feet of the settlers, their distant ancestors tried to seal up the fuel that had once seemed a miracle, and became a curse. In their wisdom and deep concern, the ancestors wished to issue a lasting warning. The pictures clearly say: danger! Keep out!

That was the intention. The problem faced by the bureaucrats was this: how to say 'Keep Out!' in a way that could be understood by any culture, even one totally ignorant of their own past and of all previous languages?

The attempt to find a solution ballooned out, through a Human Interference Task Force, to an Office of Nuclear Waste Isolation, to the Bechtel Corporation in San Francisco, until it landed in the laps of a team of specialists, among them Thomas A. Sebeok, Emeritus Professor of Linguistics and Semiotics at Bloomington, Indiana University. His brief is summarized by the title of his final report, '*Communication Measures to Bridge Ten Millennia*', which has since achieved the status of a minor cult among those intrigued by the idea of non-verbal communication.

In it, Sebeok analyses the task: to devise a message, a code and a channel of communication that guarantees both reception and understanding.

Each section of the task has its problems. Channels of communication are unreliable, because every channel is subject to the Second Law of Thermodynamics, that everything dissipates in the end. All messages decay with time and distance. A CD may last longer than a whisper or a smoke-signal, but on geological time-scales even CDs evaporate. It takes a continuous input of energy – like the building of CD cabinets and the application of cleaning devices – to keep channels of communication open and free of 'noise'.

Then there is the code, the form in which the message is couched. Words were out, because all linguistic links would have gone. CDs might encode enough information (though Sebeok's advice predated computerized CDs) – but who would bet on the survival of electric power, let alone computers, let alone compatible ones? No ideogram could work, because its conventional context would have vanished. A human figure holding up a forbidding hand could be seen as a ritual welcome. The American 'OK' sign – thumb and forefinger forming a circle – elsewhere means 'money' (in Japan), 'zero' (in France) or an obscenity (in ancient Greece).

Thirdly, reception. Any exchange of information implies an understanding between sender and receiver. And in normal exchange, the sender employs a variety of techniques to ensure understanding: gesture, repetition, synonyms and emphases. Finally, the sender usually has the assurance of feedback – a handshake, those little mm's and ah's, a nod, a glance, a thank-you note, a 'Roger'. Sagan would have no feedback, but at least he could assume joint knowledge. Sebeok was forbidden that luxury.

Sebeok had to advise that there was no solution, no foolproof way to send a message across the gulf of time into the distant future. The only possible way forward was to build a cultural bridge across the gulf, to ensure the existence of shared knowledge. The US, he advised, should establish a committee dedicated to maintaining and passing on the warning. At first, the warning would be based on hard science. But in the event of social collapse, the message would change. The committee would become an 'atomic priesthood' whose members would be guardians of a tradition that would be passed on from generation to generation, evolving with time into both an aboriginal taboo and an instruction to renew the taboo in some appropriate form.

Naturally no such 'priesthood' has ever been established, if only because the question of nuclear waste disposal has no solution. Anyway, Sebeok knew his proposal was impractical. As he concluded, even if the message survived and was understood, 'there is no assurance that future generations would obey the injunctions of the past'. The 'priesthood' might seem to be nothing more than a bunch of Jeremiahs banging on about the end of the world being nigh. Who would listen?

As for a universal script, it's an impossibility.

2

THE BEARABLE BURDEN OF SYLLABLES

Yet pictures were as essential as childhood in the evolution of writing systems. This was no simple progression, from benighted beginnings to mature enlightenment, as if the story of writing should be seen as one of those ape-to-man charts, with pictures on the left and alphabets on the right. Firstly, alphabets do not have a monopoly on intellectual accomplishment. Secondly, the idea of alphabet emerged bit by bit, edging on to the stage of history from the wings. It is worth a look at three major pre-alphabetic systems to see what they did for their cultures, and what disqualified them from direct parenthood.

To ask how ancient those predecessors were is to engage with a controversy that need not detain us here. One problem concerns the definition of writing. Some argue for a chain leading back 10,000 years to clay 'tokens' inscribed with signs that may have served as reminders to book-keepers. Some extend the chain back 30,000 years to Stone Age cave paintings and bones marked with scratches. But most agree that something of particular significance happened during the fourth millennium BC, in Mesopotamia. There, two great rivers, the Tigris and Euphrates, watered the rich plains that lay 'between the waters' (the meaning of Mesopotamia). Four increasingly complex urban societies – Sumer, Assyria, Babylonia, Elam – created several dozen cities of legendary and biblical fame, like Ur, Uruk, Nineveh and Babylon itself. In temples and palaces, produce was stored, tributes given, gifts exchanged; and all demanded records, inventories, ledger controls.

To see how necessity mothered invention, imagine a harassed temple official in Uruk on the Euphrates 200 miles south-east of today's Baghdad, some time around 3300 BC. He is surrounded by a week's income: bushels of wheat to be stored for food, fruit and vegetables for the priests' midday meal, half a dozen clay pots, a few sheep for sacrifices. And here comes a shepherd who has promised a sheep to a priest so that he can make a sacrifice to the goddess Inana to bring good weather. Except the sheep ran away, so instead he is bringing a robe made by his wife, except his wife is ill, and couldn't finish it, but he wants the priest to make the sacrifice anyway, because then the weather will be good, and then the sheep will thrive, and he will bring in another one in a week, or maybe two. And what is the priest to sacrifice, asks the official ominously, since he has no sheep? Oh, my lord, look at all these sheep, the temple has so many sheep, he could use one of these, until I repay.

How is this to be remembered? The answer is to hand – a tub of damp river clay, such as builders use for making bricks. The official does what all temple officials do, in dozens of cities up and down Mesopotamia. He grabs a handful of clay, smacks it smooth, takes a reed and uses it to indent a mark and the rough shape of a sheep. This is your mark, he says to the nervous shepherd, this is your sheep. The shepherd nods. Baked in the sun, the clay tablet will make a lasting and unforgeable record. Come to me in two weeks with your sheep, says the priest, and I will give you this clay impression of a sheep as proof that you have fulfilled your promise. If not, you may expect a visit from my extremely large assistant, who, as you know, is nowhere near as patient as I am.

Something like this must have been commonplace, for the clay tablets survive by the thousand, and some of the earliest pictures are clear: an ox's head, an ear of barley, a pig, a donkey. Eighty-five per cent of Uruk's tablets keep account of food, livestock and textiles. Obviously, it was good enough as a shorthand for priests, who knew what they were talking about. But it was an imperfect accounting system. Is the sheep income, or a debt, or outgoing? Is it alive or dead? When was the transaction agreed, when fulfilled? Such problems multiplied as wealth and complexity grew, throwing up disputes over land ownership, irrigation rights, boundaries, inheritance. A pictorial, or ideographic, system simply won't work for anything more than the most childlike forms of accounting.

So these clay tablets might have been just another dead end. But Mesopotamian cultures endured, and continuity allowed for the slow evolution of both culture and script. After some five hundred years, the system evolved into something more complex. Firstly, since drawing on clay gives a ragged line, it's neater if you use a reed to make a three-dimensional imprint – a mark that is wedge-shaped, or 'cuneiform', a word coined from the Latin *cuneus* by Oxford's professor of Hebrew and Arabic, Thomas Hyde, in 1677. Such marks were combined into geometrical abstractions of the original image.

Secondly, as the pictures – logograms, to give them their technical name – became ever more abstract, the script made a conceptual leap forward. It began to represent syllables.

To understand what this meant demands a leap into a non-literate culture, which I had a chance to do during my brief time with the Waorani in Ecuador. Until recently, they had the rare distinction of being among the fiercest tribes known to anthropologists. Some 40 per cent of all deaths were the result of revenge spearings. Few outsiders survived an encounter. Understandably, they had been an isolated group for centuries, until American missionaries tried to make contact in the late 1950s. All five were speared. But the sister of one and the wife of another, working with a Waorani woman who had fled to the outside, were inspired by the martyrdom to seek lasting contact. Since they were women, and therefore less of a threat, and since they were accompanied by a tribeswoman, they succeeded. Work started on the language, which turned out to be unrelated to any other. It took years. By the time I came along, several missionary-linguists spoke it well, and most of the tribe was living in peace. The point of this story is that to crack the language, the linguists had no help at all in their analysis from the Waorani themselves. Lacking contact with other languages, they had never had any reason to undertake the highly sophisticated business of analysing their own. They had no more idea of their own grammar than anyone else who has not been taught it. They had no word for 'word', let alone smaller units like syllables.

Linguistic analysis has a long but diffuse history. The oldest dates back to Sumer. The next, a millennium later, is a grammar of Sanskrit by Panini, written in the fifth century BC at the earliest, while western languages look back to the work of a Greek grammarian, Dionysius Thrax, in the first century BC. It took tens of thousands of years of speaking and a couple of millennia of writing before anyone got around to looking at how we do what any two-year-old can do. If, as seems increasingly likely, language is instinctive, it's hardly surprising that the sounds we make are as hard to analyse as hormones. All we see are the effects.

Language breaks into numerous elements that create and recreate meaning. First in line for analysis are words. We reorder words to show who does what to whom: The dog bit the man, the man bit the dog. Word order involves some of the most basic rules of grammar, which children pick up effortlessly. Take just one 'rule' about never ending sentences with a preposition, and then listen to this bed-time complaint by a six-year-old: *What did you bring that book I don't want to be read out of from up for?* What a wonderful nesting of thoughts, all bracketed by the opening 'what' and the final 'for'. We string words together to make new concepts, a technique which German is notoriously good at, both in real speech and in fun. I once received a car-tax reminder headed '*Kraft-fahrzeugsteuerbescheidverfahren*' (Power-travelling-tool-tax-information-proceeding), which almost matches the nonce-word for the assassin of the aunt of a Hottentot chief: *Hottentotten-potentaten-tanten-totenattentäter.* (Incidentally, that single noun, which doesn't really need the hyphens that I've thoughtfully inserted, contains not just a string of words, but many smaller units of meaning, like lots of spurious *-en's*, weak genitives, in grammatical terms, to which we shall be returning later). But words themselves are easily broken apart: In *My Fair Lady*, Eliza Doolittle sings 'abso-blooming-lutely still', carefully obeying rules which forbid her to sing 'absolute-blooming-ly still'. Such things happen in all languages. There's a German translation of Lewis Carroll's *Jabberwocky* in which the line 'and stood awhile in thought' could be rendered in a scanning translation as '*er fing zu denken an*' (he set to think out); but the need for a rhyme gives a playful twist: *er an-zu-denken-fing* (he out to-think-set).

Even a superficial glance is enough to show that words are not fundamental at all. The search for basic units leads quickly to the next element down in size: the syllable. In popular speech, that unit is about as small as you need to go. You spell things out in words of one syllable, and Macbeth metaphorically divides recorded time into syllables. In poetry, syllables carry rhyme and stress. Members of sub-cultures – children, thieves, soldiers – often play with syllables to create private languages. A well-documented one is 'back slang,' in which syllables are reversed and then made pronounceable by adding *-ay*. 'Ackbay angslay' turns out to be quite simple to master, and utterly baffling to the uninitiated: my mother-in-law, Lael Wertenbaker, a reporter with *Time* magazine, used it to avoid Nazi phonetaps when she was based in Berlin in

1940. Common sense suggests that syllables are the atoms of language (though they're not, as we shall see later).

The syllable, then, was a good starting-point for the refinement of Sumerian script. Originally, a picture could merely have suggested its name, which would change with the language, as '2' may be read as 'two', '*deux*', or '*zwei*'. At some point, some forgotten genius seems to have realized that a sign for a simple object symbolized both the object and a sound – its name. The two can be separated. Once the symbol is used to represent sound, the same symbol can be used for that sound whenever it occurs:

'2morrow and 2morrow and 2morrow . . .'

This is a sort of visual pun termed a 'rebus', short for a seventeenth-century Latin tag *non verbis sed rebus*, when meaning is captured 'not by words but by things', as in 'my voice is .' At a stroke, symbols no longer simply record objects, but *language*. Some archaeologists claim to pinpoint the town where this idea first arose: Jemdet Nasr, around 3000 BC. A Sumerian tablet found in 1926–8 contains a picture of a reed at the start of a list of temple-goods. A reed makes no sense. But the same sound (*gi*) also means 'render' or 'repay'. Some smart accountant had simply borrowed the reed sign, switched contexts, and come up with a repayment symbol.

The same principle can be applied to parts of words. 'Barley' was '*she*', with a short 'e' as in 'shepherd', so the 'barley' sign was used to begin all words starting '*she-*'. Endings worked in the same way. English does it in children's code-games. Make a bee stand for the syllable 'be-'; combine it with a picture of a leaf; and lo and behold: 'belief'.

Sentences can be built on the same pattern. As an English example, imagine six little images:

Easy, especially if you know a little English literature. But try going on with 'that is the question'. No common image can stand for the sound of 'that', because there are no one-syllable nouns that begin with a voiced 'th'. If you want to continue the game, you have to improvise. You might, for instance, devise a literary version of charades, using a sign for 'vat' and another, a so-called determinative, for 'sounds like' or 'rhymes with'.

Cuneiform was well suited to record Sumerian, because it was built on a skeleton of syllables and four vowels, modified by prefixes and suffixes. Its pictographic origins were soon lost. But a syllabic script has a staggering range of ambiguities. Like all written languages, Sumerian cuneiform had words and syllables that mixed up spelling, meaning and sound. Some were spelled differently but sounded the same (like the English *sun/son*), or spelled the same but differed in meaning (like a bird's *bill*, the name *Bill*, a *bill* for payment), or sounded the same but differed in both spelling and meaning (like the 'bill' sound in *buil*ding or a*bil*ity). Accuracy was imposed with the determinatives, specifying the concept behind the word: in 'English cuneiform', a 'bill' symbol could be followed by a bird-sign, a name-sign, or a currency-sign: or an could also mean 'ore' or 'or', with determinatives added to specify 'boat object', 'metal' or 'alternative'. Sumerian writing matched English in complexity: the same sign might be used as an ideogram, syllable or determinative.

This was a complete writing system, but for centuries it was still very limited, for technical reasons. Clay tablets could be up to a foot across to record year-end accounts. Mostly, though, they were only the size of a hand, and there was no space to record much except the most vital snippets of information. Meanwhile, we must suppose, a whole universe went unrecorded. At the courts of kings, bards sang songs of ancient heroes. In temples, priests recited prayers and sacred texts. But no one thought to make larger tablets and write these things down because the poems were passed on by word of mouth and because the purpose of writing, other than to record economic information, was to display mastery of the complex script. It was only when Sumerian started to vanish that, in about 2050 BC, King Shulgi of Ur ordered the old oral literature to be recorded, on tablets which either did not survive or have yet to be found.

Writing cuneiform to record Sumerian was quite a

challenge. But it gets worse. Another people, known as Akkadians, spread southward around the middle of the third millennium BC. By 2300 BC Akkadian was spoken all across the empire, with Sumerian as an increasingly poor relation (hence Shulgi's determination to record it), dying out as a spoken language around 2000 BC. The Akkadians adopted cuneiform, and in doing so added another dimension of complexity. Their language was Semitic (along with Hebrew, Arabic, Aramaic and many others), and had nothing in common with Sumerian, the roots and relatives of which are still unknown. The meaning of most of the Sumerian signs remained; but they were read as Akkadian. It was as if a German would read

as '*Sein oder nicht sein.*' No connection at all, except in the mind of a bilinguist. But in other instances the same signs might retain their original Sumerian sounds inside Akkadian words. To follow through the German–English transliteration, the bee- and oar-symbols would now become the first two syllables of *beordnen* (to order or summon).

After centuries of social and literary evolution, Akkadian became the lingua franca of the Mesopotamian world, adopted and modified by neighbouring cultures. The two unrelated languages, with their single writing system, endured side by side, with Akkadian the language of administration and Sumerian the language of ancient literature. Scribes had to know both. And that was hard. It took years of work, just to learn how to write. We know how hard thanks to a famous scribal exercise that was copied and recopied over centuries. It records the complaints of a schoolboy who lived in Shurrupak about 2000 BC. His father was wealthy enough to pay for tutors and provide him with the time to study. So the boy was a member of an elite class of intellectuals, as were all scribes. He became a sort of schoolboy Everyman.

All day, every day, for ten years, he sits in the 'tablethouse' on his clay-brick bench with his best friend, learning cuneiform. As a five year old, he has to practise using his stylus to imprint horizontal, vertical and sloping wedge-shapes, in two different lengths. Then he starts to learn his list of 900 signs, with some signs representing more than one syllable, and each sign sounding different in Sumerian and Akkadian. Then he moves on to drills in stringing syllables together to make words, thousands of them, all listed in various categories. It is like learning a dictionary. Like all schoolboys, this one took liberties; and the teachers kept his attention in the traditional way. In one version of the story:

The door-monitor said: 'Why did you go out without permission?' and beat me. The water-monitor said, 'Why did you take water without my permission?' and beat me. The Sumerian monitor said, 'You spoke in Akkadian!' and beat me. My teacher said, 'Your handwriting is not at all good!' and beat me . . . My teacher, reading my tablet, said, 'There's something missing!' and beat me. The man in charge of neatness said, 'You loitered in the street and didn't keep your clothes straight!' and beat me. The man in charge of silence said, 'Why did you talk without permission?' and beat me . . . So I began to hate the scribal art and neglect the scribal art. My teacher took no delight in me.

Actually, it was not all bad. The exercise ends with the boy asking his father to invite the head teacher to his home. Perhaps this is a little piece of wishful thinking for teachers, because he is showered with food, clothes and cash. In gratitude, he wishes his wayward pupil well. 'Because you have honoured me, may your pointed stylus write well for you, may your exercises contain no faults, may you walk among the highest of the school graduates.' But there is no suggestion that he ever wrote anything of interest, or grew to enjoy his labours.

Complexity piled on complexity, for some 3000 years. Two dialects evolved from Akkadian – Babylonian and Assyrian, both of which come in early and late forms. Scribes delighted in displaying their erudition by writing the same words in different ways, and in copying ancient forms of 1000, even 2000 years earlier found in libraries, rubbish dumps or private collections. A sixth-century BC king, Nabonidus, had his scribes copy tablets made by Sargon of Akkad in the twenty-third century BC.

For people used to alphabets, cuneiform seems a system of hideous complexity, crying out for reform. Yet that does not seem to have deterred the many Middle Eastern cultures that adopted it. Quite the opposite. Imagine what the Sumerian teacher would have said: Of course it's demanding! Everything worthwhile demands effort! That's just the way life is if you want to be educated and successful.

So for three millennia, successive and related cultures used cuneiform not only for practical purposes, but also to record their greatest cultural achievements. Akkadian kings commissioned scribes to transcribe the poetry that told them of their heroic ancestors. The most famous of the epics concerned the hero, Gilgamesh, who had sought the secret of immortality from the immortal Uta-napishti and heard from him the story of how he, Uta-napishti, survived a great Flood by building a boat. The greatest collection of tablets was that of the last king of Assyria, Ashurbanipal, an avid collector of tablets old and newly written, including several versions of the Gilgamesh epic which were buried beneath the ruins of the royal libraries when Nineveh was burned by invaders in 612 BC.

There they lay until unearthed by a British team in the 1850s, revealing a treasure to amaze the world: a previously unknown civilization that long predated the

Greeks. But it took years to assess these finds, and the tens of thousands of other tablets that now form the British Museum's stupendous collection. When in 1872 a young cuneiformist, George Smith, realized what he held in his hands, the discovery drove him wild: 'I am the first man to read that after two thousand years of oblivion!' he muttered, then, as E. A. Wallis Budge describes the scene in a history of cuneiform studies, Smith put the tablet down 'and began to rush about the room in a great state of excitement, and to the astonishment of those present, began to undress himself'.

Gilgamesh astounded the Victorians partly because it cast new light on the Bible, partly because it is also one of the world's great epics. Its verse is proof not only of Akkadian literary talent – though it must be a minute fraction of a 'literature' existing mostly in oral form – but also of the ability of cuneiform to capture poetic language in writing.

My own discovery of *Gilgamesh*, in the first Penguin edition, was a minor teenage epiphany. I force-fed friends, ancient-mariner-fashion, and probably lost a few. The bit that put a catch in my throat was when Uta-napishti, the Akkadian Noah in his ark, realizes the storm that caused the Flood is abating:

> The ocean grew calm, that had thrashed like a
>   woman in labour,
> The tempest grew still, the Deluge ended.

> I looked at the weather, it was quiet and still,
> But all the people had turned to clay.
> The flood plain was flat like the roof of a house.
> I opened a vent, on my cheeks fell the sunlight.
>
> Down sat I, I knelt, and I wept,
> Down my cheeks the tears were coursing.

I loved the image: *all the people had turned to clay*. This, by the way, is from the new translation by Andrew George, Reader in Assyriology at London's School of Oriental and African Languages. Actually, I am still nostalgic for the line in the version I first knew: 'all *mankind* was turned to clay', but Andrew George tells me that's a little too free.

There is more to these images and sentiments than I appreciated. Don't you warm to Uta-napishti, especially when you compare him to Noah? Noah comes out of his adventure a bit self-satisfied, glorying in his god and his own virtue, in the secure knowledge that his fellows deserved to be turned to clay because they were bad. Uta-napishti knows himself to be a victim, for the Flood was unleashed by a goddess lashing out in anger at the other gods, and she regrets it bitterly: 'How could I declare a war to destroy my people? It is I who give birth, these people are mine! And now, like fish, they fill the ocean!' Uta-napishti's first reaction might have been to accuse, or grovel, or give thanks for his survival. Instead, he mourns for the innocent dead, for a universe which is the plaything of deities as perverse and petty as humans. The images and feelings have an immediacy and a humanity that seem independent of time, cultures, and language.

I hope by now you can see the outlines of a conclusion – that non-alphabetical scripts do not necessarily limit literary flair or emotional responses. Whatever separates the two systems – non-alphabetical and alphabetical – is to be sought in more than the alphabet's greater efficiency and simplicity. A script's survival seems to depend more on the nature of the culture, on the materials used and on the determination of its scribes to preserve it and transmit it unchanged down the generations.

Let's see how this idea works out by looking at the second great writing system of the ancient Middle East, Egyptian hieroglyphic.

Until the early nineteenth century, Egyptian writing had been a mystery for 2000 years. In the first century BC, a Greek historian Diodorus Siculus visited Egypt. The writing was still in use then, though much overlaid by Graeco-Roman culture. The locals, he said disparagingly, called their script hieroglyphs, 'sacred writing', but it wasn't real writing because it only used pictures. Four hundred years later, the hieroglyphic script was as dead as its religion. The world was left only with the enigmatic evidence of a vanished culture. As the Bible rose in eminence, so Egypt's reputation for intellectual achievement declined. Hieroglyphs were seen not as elements of a script but as symbols of an impenetrable and mystical paganism. At best, this fed into a romantic belief in a pre-Babel unity, a single language which represented pure thought, a perfect mode of communication. So attempts at understanding hieroglyphic focused on deconstructing the signs as symbols for ideas. The belief in a mystical Egypt dominated European attitudes in the late eighteenth century. Mozart drew on it for *The Magic Flute* in 1791; Napoleon, whose Egyptian campaigns opened in 1798, adopted the bee as his personal symbol because it was supposedly the sign for 'ruler' in hieroglyphic.

It was, of course, Napoleon's campaign that marked a turning point. The time was right, for already a Danish scholar had pointed out that the total number of symbols then known – about 1000 – was far too few to encode a whole vocabulary. In July 1799, workmen extending the fortifications of el-Rashid – also known as Rosetta – found a 762-kg stone with an inscription in three scripts, Greek, hieroglyphic, and a flowing one later recognized as demotic, a written form of hieroglyphic. The find was immediately recognized as a treasure, for it was a bi-lingual, and tri-scriptorial, version of the same text. A couple of weeks later, it reached the French scholars running the Egyptian Institute in Cairo. After England's defeat of the French, the stone was reluctantly surrendered to the victors, who carried it to London, where it remains today as the centre-piece of the British Museum's Egyptian collection.

Work on decipherment, perhaps the most famous of all decipherments, started at once. It took twenty years, involving several orientalists, in particular the Englishman Thomas Young, a polymath of such legendary genius that as a schoolboy he was nicknamed 'Phenomenon', and the equally brilliant young Frenchman Jean-François Champollion, who delivered his first lecture on Egyptology at the age of 16. Both were held up by their assumption that they were dealing with a collection of symbols, of 'ideograms', not a script that could be read phonetically. Progress was marked by intense rivalry between the two and several vituperative disputes about primacy, all mixed with grudging mutual admiration. In 1822, when he was still only 32, Champollion read the first paper announcing a partial solution to the problem. He had identified some letters among the 'ideograms'. Other publications followed in 1824 and 1828, in which Champollion effectively solved the remaining problems of decipherment. In 1832, after returning from a trip to Egypt, he died. He was still only 41.

Like cuneiform, hieroglyphic was rooted in pictures, devised about 3300 BC. It seems an odd coincidence that two close cultures should develop writing at roughly the same time. Many historians think it is too much of a coincidence, and that the idea of writing diffused from

Mesopotamia to the Nile. Perhaps Egyptian traders, ambassadors or warriors carried the message home: guess what – those guys send messages by making marks on bits of clay.

However it happened, Egyptians adapted pictures and moved to 'proper' writing by way of the rebus principle. But unlike cuneiform, hieroglyphic was initially cut into, or painted on rock, and not limited by the size of the note-pad or the shape of the writing instrument. Egyptians could take all the space they needed and experiment with any shape in writing that became more art-form than record. A wavy line depicting water, the word for which sounded something like *net* in Ancient Egyptian, came to stand for the sound of '*n*'. An owl (perhaps something like *mu*) became '*m*', a loaf of bread, *ta*, was a '*t*'. More about the letters later, because it may be of significance for the origin of our alphabet that the Egyptians had their own individual letters mixed in with some 700 signs for objects, consonant groups, phonetic complements (which reinforced other similar-sounding signs) and determinatives. As in cuneiform, the 100 or so common determinatives clarified ambiguities. Thus the symbols

(writing materials) + (bookroll determinative) = writing

while,

(writing materials) + (seated man determinative) = scribe.

Many determinatives add one of several related meanings, leaving the context to click the final meaning into place. The word *nefret* could mean a beautiful woman, a type of crown or a cow, depending on its final determinative. One sign added the sense of eat, drink, speak, think or feel. A bird sign had the sense of 'flying thing' and also implied 'insect'.

All these practices combined to make a system that was rich enough to carry any amount of meaning, with many redundancies and different forms. From the start, the script came in two versions: in mainstream hiero-glyphic, which was mainly carved on monuments; and in hieratic, abbreviated almost abstract versions of the same signs used for business and personal purposes on papy-rus. Later, from about 600 BC, scribes used demotic, a further abbreviated script that looks like modern short-hand. Sometimes single letters were reinforced by two- or three-consonantal signs, or more than one determi-native was used to be extra-sure. Take the word for 'cat', a particularly charming example because the old Egyptian for 'cat' was pronounced *miaow*, or something like it. Egyptians wrote it as ░░░░, which transliterates as *mj-j-w-cat sign*. The *mj* syllable meant 'milk-jug', though the apparent link was a coincidence. Then comes another '*j*', a phonetic complement to reinforce the first (hidden) '*j*'. Then a '*w*' and a 'small feline' determinative. Indeed, there was such an excess of symbols that scribes were free to play with them.

Sometimes, scribes would deliberately misspell words, or reverse letters, or overprint to form monograms.

The system's richness and flexibility led to a final florescence. Signs multiplied, from about 700 in classical Egyptian times (*c.* 2000–1500 BC) to some 5000 in the century or two before hieroglyphic fell from use in AD 400. Scribes created variants for fun, or to be deliberately obscure. In a famous hymn in the temple of Esna to the ram-god Khnum, every single sign is a ram, with the sense dictated by the determinatives. This must have been considered a terribly clever, perhaps witty, way of asserting that Khnum was omni-present. An elite playing academic games – it was that sort of thing that helped create the impression among outsiders that the whole system was vastly exotic and mysterious.

In fact, experts can read hieroglyphic pretty fluently. This has nothing to do with its embedded alphabet. Richard Parkinson, Assistant Keeper in the Department of Egyptian Antiquities at the British Museum, points out that this is precisely because it is *not* purely alphabetical that it is so legible – 'you can tell at a glance what category a word belongs to. It is remarkably efficient, and really straightforward.' Egyptian scribes would have agreed. In the fourth century BC, perhaps under the influence of the Greek alphabet, a stele was made in Naucratis using only consonantal signs, and is far harder to read than ordinary hieroglyphic with its mixed orthography.

Still, it was never easy. So much Egyptian writing survives that a tourist might conclude that it permeated all society. Far from it. As a rule-of-thumb, Egyptologists assume that less than 1 per cent of the population could read, and a good deal less of them write well. For that tiny percentage, it was a vital occupation, the products of which were for display, but the techniques of which were best kept close to the chest. For they were the government, and it was the ability to write that defined their identity.

Set your heart to writings!

urged the master scribe and author, Khety, in Richard Parkinson's translation.

Observe how it rescues from labour!
Look, there is no excelling writings –
They are a watertight boat! . . .
I shall make you love writing more than your
    mother.
I shall make its beauties be shown to you.
Now, it is greater than any other profession.
There is not its like in the land.

Writing served the priestly agenda: to buttress the privileged position of the elite servants of the godhead, the pharaoh. It was not exactly in their interests to bring writing downmarket.

Yet hints of a more populist literature, perhaps an oral tradition, survive. Rich Egyptians liked to adorn their tombs with inscriptions known as funerary autobiographies in which the dead man regales passers-by with his life story, in an idealized form that emphasizes his virtues. One, however, escaped the confines of the grave. It is the story of a courtier, Sinuhe, who was a middle-ranking official in the service of the queen, Nefru, when her husband, the 12th-Dynasty pharaoh Amenemhet, was assassinated. Believing himself to be a potential victim in the civil war he thinks is bound to follow, Sinuhe falls into a blind panic and flees to northern Palestine, the area known to Egyptians as Retenu, where, in the end, he flourishes. But he is in constant turmoil about his inexplicable fear, which drove him from the presence of his god-king – Amenemhet's successor, Senusret – into a life outside Egypt, lacking meaning and identity. Eventually, he is summoned home and forgiven. Irrationality and chaos are banished and he enters upon a revered old age which ends in a favoured tomb.

Perhaps the most telling language is when Sinuhe has to explain his panic-stricken flight to his lord and master, and cannot:

> This flight which your humble servant made –
> I had not planned it. It was not in my heart.
> I had not thought of it. I know not what parted
>   me from my place.

It was like the nature of a dream . . .
I had no cause to be afraid; no one had run
  after me.
I had heard no reproaches; my name had not
  been heard in the herald's mouth.
Only – that shuddering of my limbs,
My feet hastening,
My heart overmastering me,
The God who fated this flight dragging me
  away!

The Tale of Sinuhe, in this translation by Richard Parkinson,
captures something deeply significant about Egyptian
society: the fear of death, the agony of separation from that
which promises to conquer death: the pharaoh, Egypt
herself – and the blessing of returning to both.

Again, an epic poem indicates that, even if elitism,
tradition and technical limitations imposed limits, there
was nothing in the script itself that constrained literacy.

Both hieroglyphic and cuneiform contribute to the seed-
bed from which the alphabet sprang. Chinese, the early
history of which overlaps both the other two in time, has
no direct connection with the alphabet, but it does throw
light on why an alphabet might appeal to fringe cultures,
and why a system as demanding as Chinese outstayed

both its Middle Eastern contemporaries.

How and when the Chinese acquired writing is a controversy that need not detain us. Perhaps they invented it from scratch (literally: the earliest Chinese writings were divinations scratched on tortoise-shells and the shoulder-bones of cattle). Or perhaps they got the idea by diffusion from Mesopotamia, and then improvised. However it happened, by about 1400 BC, China had a script from which modern Chinese arose. The same principles govern both: some 1500 characters from the Shang dynasty (from the seventeenth century BC to about 1025 BC) are still recognizable. The script was then used for inscriptions on bronze and for writing on bamboo, wood, silk and, finally, around AD 200, on paper. The invention of block printing in about AD 600 and then of movable-type printing – five centuries before Gutenberg independently invented it in Europe – led to an explosion of publications. Before 1900 (according to an estimate by John de Francis), Chinese printed matter exceeded that of all the rest of the world combined.

Chinese script records a variety of dialects and languages. But, contrary to a popular belief, it imposes unity only in the way Latin script 'unifies' French and Spanish. Mandarin is now standard, but to speak and read it a Cantonese has to step outside Canton's own script and dialect. Regional variation and historical change make continuities hard to follow, unless you track through each successive variation. The Shang characters for 'eye' and 'mouth' are clearly pictographic, but their modern equivalents are not.

Now to the underlying principles. It is widely believed, even by Chinese, that the language is picture-based, or ideographic. It isn't, at least not now, and probably never was, given that using pictures alone works for only simple communications. Tradition declares that there are five principles in operation: ancient pictographs, followed by three ways of combining signs that include the use of rebuses (like the character *xiang* 象 meaning 'elephant' which is also used to write *xiang* meaning 'image'), and finally additions that refine meanings – *ma* meaning 'horse' 马 also represents *ma* meaning 'mother' 妈, with a determinative for 'female' added to avoid ambiguity, while a third *ma*, meaning 'to scold or swear,' comes out as: 骂 mouth+mouth+horse (with its overtones of femininity – not politically correct, perhaps, but the original meanings are long forgotten).

Over time, the determinatives increased, from 34 per cent of signs in Shang times to 97 per cent today. So striking is this progression that some analysts prefer a different approach to the underlying principles, grouping them into three sequential stages: the ancient pictograms (a mere 1 per cent now); a mixed stage in which the same symbol stood for different but similar words (like 'I/eye'), and the same symbol for different words with related meanings (like 'eye' and 'see'); and a final stage, represented by the 97 per cent of signs which sort out ambiguities with determinatives.

One final trait is unique to Chinese. In evolving the scripts, scribes adopted the technique of welding the two main elements – determinative and root word – to form a single diagram. In hieroglyphic and cuneiform, by contrast, the determinative acts as a separate unit. So, from an early stage, Chinese script was governed by an aesthetic ideal: that all signs must be confined into their own square spaces regardless of complexity. It is as if every alphabetically based word from 'I' to 'floccinaucinihilipilification' had to fit into a rectangle of the same length.

It is hard to unravel the evolution of tens of thousands of signs modified by millions of scholars over three thousand years or so and, until recently, no one in China or outside had much idea of how the task of reading was accomplished. Now, many specialists hold that the phonetic (sound) elements are fundamental, with semantic (meaning) elements added. It is possible to recast almost all Chinese characters into a matrix, with 214 semantic signs down one side and some 4000 phonetic signs along the top. That produces 800,000 'syllable' boxes, far more than necessary to record all known Chinese characters. In fact, you can do a pretty good job with 'only' 895 phonetic signs, producing 4300 characters, which is about as many as most literate people need.

Now, it's certainly tough for Chinese children to master a system the intricacies of which very few of their teachers and parents understand, and acquire a working knowledge of tens of thousands of 'symbols'. But it's not as bad as it is believed to be in the west, where most people think that a scholar has to master tens of thousands of characters, all of which are isolates. If this were so, Chinese could not read unfamiliar signs, which they do often because each sign is written and read in a certain order, from top left to bottom right.

Also, if all signs really *were* unique ideograms, it would be impossible to write foreign names. In fact, literate Chinese write foreign names pretty well. They do so by selecting signs which roughly represent the word, syllable by syllable. My own name is relatively easy. John comes out as Yue Han, and depending on the tone, *man* means either 'conceal' or 'satisfying', and can be written accordingly, with the context making it obvious that a name is intended and emptying it of the original meaning. Once on a train in Inner Mongolia a Chinese asked me, in halting English, about the famous Englishman 'Chuo-ji'. My mind was a blank. He explained, as if to an idiot. 'Great leader! The war!' At last I got it:

'Churchill?'*

'Yes. Great man. Why you no make him king?'

To non-Chinese, Chinese is an erratic, inefficient, demanding and unduly complex way of recording

---

* 'Churchill' in Chinese, transliterated in *pinyin*, is *qiu-ji-er* – 邱吉尔 a classical surname + 'lucky' + 'you'.

sounds. Obviously, the alphabetic system is easier. So why didn't Chinese simply succumb?

One simple answer is that it works, with a richness that matches or exceeds any other system. It would be ludicrous to assert otherwise, given the chronological depth, the sheer weight of writing, the intellectual and artistic range, the vast numbers of translations from other languages. Technically, it is in some ways no more complex than English, with its notorious spellings and malleable pronunciations. In both, many sounds inter-relate with many symbols, or syllables. Ostensibly, an alphabet confers a one-to-one relationship between sound and symbol. It doesn't work like that, of course. There's more to be said about the tortuous orthography of English in Chapter 4, but as a foretaste: we spell one sound of 'o' in ten different ways (so, sew, sow, oh, owe, dough, doe, beau, soak, soul) and use the same letter 'o' to represent six different sounds (so, to, on, honey, horse, and woman). So why (a baffled Chinese student might ask) doesn't *English* simply succumb to a more rational system?

Because neither is directly in competition with the other, and both occupy their own universe, as certain problems of translation can reveal. Douglas Hofstadter, the cognitive-science polymath author of the Pulitzer Prize-winning *Gödel, Escher, Bach*, tells a story of his Chinese translator, professor Wu Yunzeng. Faced by one of Hofstadter's more complex word-games, Professor

Wu compared it to a palindrome, a word or sentence that reads the same backwards and forwards. Yes, Chinese have palindromes, too. Professor Wu quoted one: *Ye luo tian luo ye*, which means, roughly, 'In autumn, the leaves fall.' Of course, to English eyes, it isn't a proper palindrome – the words read both ways, but the letters don't. Then Hofstadter presented the famous English palindrome summarizing Ferdinand de Lesseps's idea to link the Atlantic to the Pacific: 'A man, a plan, a canal – Panama!' Professor Wu was baffled. 'Panama! – canal a, plan a, man A.' It made no sense at all.

Hofstadter built a bridge between the two separate universes as follows: If you wish to preserve both literal word-by-word meaning and the word-play, you could say 'leaves fall season fall leaves'. By chance, in American English, 'fall' has two senses and so does 'leaves', leading to a wonderful solution: 'Fall leaves as soon as leaves fall.' Of course, it's not an English palindrome. But let's not quibble. Just try creating a 'proper' palindrome that would work both in English and Chinese.

The exercise opens a whole area of philosophical discussion about what is meant by translation, and how these different cultural dimensions can be made to interrelate. Perhaps they can't. Perhaps a Chinese chair, or even a French one, is too heavy with local references ever to become an English chair. Perhaps translation is always more or less 'lost in an art' (as that anagram of 'translation' would be if you tried to translate it).

Anyway, the two language-universes endure, sublimely indifferent to such concerns, each as rich as the other. Only the ignorant and arrogant would put one down from the perspective of the other.

It is the very depth and range of Chinese writing that points to a deeper reason for its survival: cultural inertia. Or if you prefer a less pejorative term, conservatism. Better still, momentum. Sheer bulk – of writing, population, geographical extent – has ensured that China has more cultural momentum than any other. In stability and endurance, it is unique. Though China often divided and fought against itself, each warring kingdom derived its values from the whole, and each new dynasty claimed the 'mandate of heaven'. Rulers, whether of empires or statelets, all relied on bureaucracies sustained by writing. Century upon century, scholars and bureaucrats accumulated learning and records in prodigious quantities. One year alone, AD 983, saw the publication of an encyclopaedia with 1000 chapters and a 250,000-page collection of basic Buddhist texts. Success generated success: some non-Chinese cultures – Korea, Japan, Vietnam – adopted Chinese script, while others made up their own versions (the 6600 characters devised by the Tanguts, who ruled north-west China for two centuries around the turn of the first millennium, have only been partially deciphered). All East Asia bowed to China's cultural dominance.

All the lynchpins of this vast and enduring edifice fed back to reinforce each other: the social order from emperor to serf, authority, scholarship, literature, art, history, writing – everything that made China the most eminent of cultures. To improve or change individual written signs was fair comment; to criticize the writing system as a whole would have been sacrilege. No one did, until this century, when the coming of the computer lightened the burden of history.

In this review of three major syllabic systems – cuneiform, hieroglyphic and Chinese – conservatism (momentum, inertia, whichever you prefer) emerges as a major force in the retention of traditional scripts. In all three, you can feel history weighing on literate elites. It is not the endurance of the scripts that demands explanation, but the endurance of the societies that used them. Once in existence, writing systems have extraordinary resilience. Change, it seems, does not arise spontaneously from within. Something has to happen to release a new creative impulse. This may be imposed on sceptical literati from above (which happened later in Korea, Turkey, Central Asia and Mongolia). Otherwise, new scripts like the early alphabet can only have a chance in some new environment, where tradition holds no sway.

To summarize these ideas, consider three propositions. Let's call them the three Working Theories of Script Evolution:

1 In a writing system, complexity knows no bounds and imposes none.
2 A writing system will last as long as its culture, unless changed by force.
3 New writing systems emerge only in new, young, ambitious cultures.

It's the third proposition that is of interest to those who seek the roots of our alphabet. If it is true, we should be on the look-out for the cultural equivalent of the tiny fossils that indicate the existence of mammals during the time of dinosaurs. For a century now, archaeologists have sought that shadowy entity, *Alphabeticus originalis*. Now, evidence has emerged to suggest it's been found.

3

LETTERS IN THE WILDERNESS

Those who seek the alphabet's origins seek a great prize: one of the major roots of western identity. Not many ever doubted that the Greek alphabet, the parent of our own, was taken over from the Phoenician (also the source of Hebrew and Arabic scripts). But this was no solution. In the words of the British archaeologist, Alan Gardiner, in 1916: 'It has been universally recognized that so simple, and therefore so perfect, an instrument for the visible recording of language could not conceivably have resulted from one spontaneous effort of genius. Cruder and more primitive methods of writing must obviously have preceded it.' The alphabet doesn't look all that simple and perfect nowadays, and readers of cuneiform, hieroglyphic or Chinese would object to such alphabetical supremacism, but he was right about the cruder precedents. From those sources, or that single source, grew imitation and descendant scripts galore; and ultimately the millions upon millions of tons of today's alphabetical writings. To be the first to identify the starting-point of an invention that would underpin the cultures of three-quarters of the whole world: it's a prize worth having.

How, when, and where did it all start? As the great discoveries in Mesopotamia, the Aegean and Egypt over the last 150 years have shown, there weren't many possibilities: Mesopotamian cuneiform, or Minoan, or Hittite, or the old Cretan or Cypriot scripts, or Egyptian hieroglyphic. Egypt was always a strong candidate. It seemed too much of a coincidence that the Egyptians should have had an alphabet embedded in their writing system for a couple of thousand years and the Phoenicians just happened to come up with the idea from scratch, in places that had traded with Egypt for centuries. Was that it? Or was there a missing link between the Egyptians and Phoenicians?

In the 1990s there emerged a possible answer. The hard evidence is minute: a few pounds of ceramics, a few small statues, rock-hewn graffiti, marks on bits of pots – the remains are as slight and as puzzling as the few bits of fossilized bone from which palaeontologists derive human origins. Though some letter-shapes leap out with startling familiarity, meaning remains a blank, and for the most part events and people pass like shadows, except for occasional flashes of insight granted by inscriptions. But there is enough here to trace the alphabet's story, from Egypt through Sinai to Palestine and Phoenicia.

West of Thebes, Egypt's ancient capital on the Nile, beyond the Valley of the Kings, the burial ground of pharaohs, ancient tracks lead up over an escarpment to the bare, brown *gebel*, the hills and valleys carved into the Western Desert by centuries of wind and rain. In 1990, a young Egyptologist from Yale, John Darnell, was working in Thebes as Senior Epigrapher for Egypt's Epigraphic Survey, based in Luxor. He had been there the previous season and had become intrigued by the tracks. A German expedition at the end of the nineteenth century and two British ones in the 1930s had recorded palaeolithic tools and some inscriptions, but no one now seemed to know much about the sites or the tracks. One was known as the Alabaster Road, because locals used to collect the creamy rock to carve into knick-knacks for tourists. It was well eroded, and had obviously been used for millennia. What had drawn people to the grim landscape above? One weekend, he and his wife, Deborah, an Egyptologist in her own right, started exploring, taking a cab to the foot of the escarpment and climbing up into the rolling desert hills.

Even on their first walk up this well-worn path, an hour and half into the desert, the Darnells stumbled on an archaeological treasure-trove. Bits of pottery by the hundred. Dressed stone blocks. The ruins of a sandstone temple built in the 17th Dynasty, about 1640 BC (though these Second Intermediate Period dates are uncertain and confusing, because dynasties overlapped). A broken stele, one of those slab-like pillars ancient Egyptians put up to record anything of significance, on which there was a winged sun-disc. And numerous inscriptions, done over many centuries, but with the time around 2000 BC emerging as a high-point of activity. For archaeologists this was almost virgin territory. The British expeditions in the 1930s had had their work cut short by the war, and no archaeologists had come since. Traditionally, Egyptologists had paid scant attention to the desert, because the ancient Egyptians had built close to the Nile. But this track, swooping over the high *gebel* and through rain-cut wadis, had once been a busy thoroughfare, part of a 40-mile short-cut across the great half-circle, the Qena Bend, which the Nile makes north of Luxor. The Darnells had in effect stumbled on an archaeological equivalent of an open-cast gold-mine.

The following season, they explored further along the valley, and found more – some odd signs which didn't look like anything John had seen before, except in pictures, and another stele dating from the 13th Dynasty (about 1780–1650 BC) cut into the rockface. To the inexperienced eye, the signs didn't look like much. But if as John suspected they dated from around 2000 BC, the word 'significant' hardly did them justice. It made no sense to read them as Egyptian. The only other signs like them that he had seen were copies of some in the Sinai desert, which formed a script known as Proto-Sinaitic. Like the Proto-Sinaitic signs, the new discoveries seemed to be letters, possibly the earliest examples yet of the letters that would one day form the basis of the Phoenician alphabet, then the Greek, then the Latin. Even at that first glance – was that an early version of the letter *a*? And here a sort of *m*? – he realized he could be staring at the very roots of the alphabet.

They checked their discovery against the records. The area they had 'discovered' had been visited in 1936 by Hans Winkler on one of the British expeditions. He had noted its name – the Wadi el-Hol, the Valley of Terror – and recorded the 13th-Dynasty stele, but few other details. Now they had been there, the Darnells could see that his black-and-white pictures showed some of the same mass of rock-hewn inscriptions. These and everything else would have to be photographed in detail. Pottery and smaller inscribed stones would need to be brought back to Thebes for research and conservation. The 'letters', if that was what they were, would demand their own research project. Who made them? Why? And once work started, the site would need protection from theft. Thieves are the most notorious and destructive scourge of Egypt's relics, and a gang boss can earn tens of thousands of dollars from tourists and dealers for a few days' work by his minions. To such people, the whole area was a pile of money, just lying in the desert. The Darnells needed to move fast. They approached authorities, wrote proposals, received backing. The Theban Desert Road Survey was born, and work started on the temple area at the Luxor end of the road.

In 1993, they made their first official trip deeper into the desert to the Wadi el-Hol. They were in two cars, each with a driver, approaching from the north via a point where 4 × 4s could climb up on to the *gebel*. John, with his work gear and a spiked stick – a *shuba* – which he usually brought along in case of trouble, was in the lead, with the Chief Inspector of Antiquities. Deborah followed. Approaching the wadi, they both felt the same tingle of anticipation, suddenly intensified by the unnerving sight of tyre-tracks. Someone else had been here not long before. Hemmed in by the walls of the curving valley, they rounded a spur, and saw, to their astonishment, a tractor with a flatbed trailer.

Several men in long cotton shifts were in mid-robbery. Deborah felt a violent rush of adrenaline. 'All I can compare it to is if you were to come home and there was somebody beating up your children.' Three of the men were off up the side of the valley, sizing up likely inscriptions, while two were actually at work hacking at the 13th-Dynasty stele carved into the rock face.

The cars stopped. The men hardly had a second to stare

because John exploded from his car, *shuba* in hand. The men ran, clumsily, hauling at their shifts and dropping them before sprinting away up the wadi, clad only in underpants and sandals, with John in pursuit.

'Wait!' shouted the inspector to John.

Deborah was out of her car now. 'But we have to do something!' Five against five. She had a vision of instant arrests.

'No, wait!' Up the wadi, John paused. 'We have to get back and report this to the police.'

He was right. There was no chance of an arrest there and then. But if they just left, the thieves would return and continue their destructive work and cart away their booty. At least they could prevent that. Using an archaeological pick, John popped a hole in the tractor's fuel tank and knocked the tyre valves off with his *shuba*. Seething with indignation and frustration, they gathered the discarded tools – chisels, razor-wire, mallets – to forestall destruction out of mere vengeance. They started to check the damage. It was not random. Someone had marked likely slabs of hieroglyphic with little white arrows. Luckily, no one had been interested in the odd squiggles of Proto-Sinaitic, if that's what they were. They ran their fingers over the stele, hardly touched when they came first, now a wreck. You'd think they'd know they'd get a better price if they cut it carefully, but they had just hacked at it.

Just then, another Antiquities policeman arrived on a

motorbike to check on the expedition. Soon, he had back-up. Sense prevailed. A couple of the abandoned shifts contained ID cards. The tractor had a registration number. Policemen scribbled things in pads. These people could be traced.

That experience defined the context of the Darnells' work over the next four seasons. The thieves were arrested, and bailed, and returned to the valley several times. The police were responsible for security, but were hindered in their ability to provide protection by the remoteness and vastness of the site. It was impossible to patrol several miles of rock face, or cordon it off. Yet their job forced them to impose restrictions on the Darnells. There could be no work without permits and escorts. Every trip was an epic of form-filling, weaving through a bureaucratic maze of antiquities departments, local police and criminal investigators, all leading to an expedition of several cars and motorbikes, and a dozen or more men, most of whom had nothing to do.

This astonishing site; the thieves; the police; the urgent need for research – all combined to catch the archaeologists in unresolvable paradoxes. Ideally, the work should have been done with discretion, at leisure. But that was no longer an option. Now the material had to be catalogued, researched and reported as quickly as possible to prevent further losses. Besides, they didn't want any academics to accuse them of deliberately holding back. But to announce the finds would open the place to further depredation from thieves, tourists, even other archaeologists eager for a share, with the only consolation that publicity made it harder to sell the stuff, and so conferred protection.

In several hectic seasons in the two main sites – the Wadi el-Hol and the temple area they named Gebel Antef after the temple's 17th-Dynasty builder – John and Deborah recorded everything that survived, even as it was plundered. The stele, carved in the reign of Sobekhotep III, went, bit by bit. An inscription in which someone had quoted from the *Tale of Sinuhe*, vital for making comparisons with other later versions, gone for ever, existing now only in John's photographs and copies. Other inscriptions scrawled over out of pure malice. Sherds scrunched over by patrolmen or taken into custody for months.

Their records allowed the Darnells to propose a context for the remains. The 'road' was one of a network that linked Thebes to towns to the north, in particular to the even older necropolis of Abydos, and to oases in the Libyan desert. Previously no one had suspected that the Egyptians had ventured much into the desert. But here was evidence that the road was in use for over a millennium, from 'Dynasty 0' (before 300 BC). Runners and then pony-express riders carried mail, pharaohs journeyed back and forth, officials came and went, desert policemen patrolled, priests made astronomical observations. The text of the vanishing stele, carved in the written form of hieroglyphic, hieratic, made clear that it was cut during the reign of the

13th-Dynasty king Sobekhotep, around 1750 BC, who, in John's words, 'describes himself as driving back foreign hordes in the desert and going sleepless and hungry training desert watchmen'. One intriguing text refers to people 'spending the day beneath this mountain on holiday'. They may have paused here to venerate the goddess Hathor.

To archaeologists, one of the most interesting of the Darnells' findings was a record of the pre-dawn (heliacal) rising of Sirius, a star central to Egyptian religion. Sothis, as the Egyptians called Sirius the 'Dog Star', is also central to Egyptian chronology, because its heliacal rising was supposed to coincide with New Year's Day, but in fact only did so only once every 1460 years or so. This epochal event was recorded in AD 139, and must therefore also have occurred in about 1321 BC, 2781 BC, and so on. But so far references to these dates are lacking, as is any secure base for a chronology before about 600 BC. An accurate record of a 'Sothic' rising, whatever the time of year, would be a godsend. This reading, apparently made during the 17th Dynasty, early in the sixteenth century BC, will, if it is substantiated, help in providing a fixed point for the dating of Egyptian history.

And then there are those few intriguing letters. Darnell makes a forthright claim: they are not only 'early alphabetical inscriptions', they 'are the earliest we thus far have'. From the shape of the letters, the writing seemed to run from right to left. Twelve marks suggest links between Egyptian writing and later Semitic letters, including an ox-head, an eye, a house, a snake, and water. In these and other signs, Darnell sees the roots of our own *a, b, r, n, m, p, w*, and *t*, and four Semitic letters. Some combinations suggest Semitic words, like *rb* (chief), though it is impossible to be certain without knowing what sounds the signs represent. The origins of the signs, Darnell suggests, lie both in hieroglyphic and in its abbreviated cursive form known as hieratic. One sign, for instance, is of a seated man with a zigzag flourish underneath. What this might mean in Semitic, if it is indeed being used as a Semitic letter, is anyone's guess. But in Egyptian writing it is a determinative indicating that the subject is a person. This version with the zigzag is a form rare in hieroglyphs but common in hieratic.

There is no doubt in Darnell's mind of the importance of his discovery. In 1997, he went public with his findings in general terms, in articles, lectures and press releases. Academic support came from several sources, principally Chip Dobbs-Allsopp, a Semitic language expert at the Princeton Theological seminary, and Kyle McCarter, Professor of Near Eastern Studies at Johns Hopkins University. Even as Darnell was preparing his material for a more extended academic presentation, he e-mailed me his conclusions: 'One of the most significant features of these inscriptions is that, by blending cursive and non-cursive forms, they have allowed me to identify the point in time during the development of the Egyptian script when the early alphabetic signs would have split off.' That split occurred, by his reckoning, during the late First Intermediate Period or early Middle Kingdom, which means, on current dating systems, about 2000–1900 BC: 'The letters I am typing now derive from the collaborative efforts of Egyptians and Western Asiatics around the year Y2K BC.'

The key people are the 'Asiatics', foreigners from today's Israel, Syria, Lebanon and Jordan who had been in Egypt from long before 2000 BC. The term was applied by Egyptians to virtually anyone from east of Suez. They often reviled these outsiders, with their beards, kilts and long braided hair. Some of the 'kilt-wearers' seem to have been from the walled trading towns of Palestine: Byblos, Ashkelon, Gezer, Jericho. Some came to trade, others to work. But there were those of a different type, shaggy bowmen who lived as semi-nomads in the wilds and entered Egypt either as marauders or prisoners. They were as much a threat to the settled and civilized Egyptians as the Mongols were later to the settled and civilized Chinese. And the two seem to have lived on similar terms, reviling each other, yet needing each other. On the one side lay wealth and goods beyond measure; on the other, slaves for armies and building projects, and raw material.

Egyptian rulers needed peace in the borderlands of Sinai to keep access to its turquoise mines. They needed wood from the great cedar forests of Lebanon. Trade and strategy demanded that the routes east and north-east be secured against the 'wild men of Asia'.

This was not always easy. Dynasties declined and fell, other powers seized their chance. In one such period around the end of the third millennium BC, barbarian invasions menaced the Nile Valley. 'Lo, the vile Asiatic!' warned Akhtoy, a 10th-Dynasty pharaoh who wrote a book of instruction on statecraft. 'He never dwells in one place but has been forced to stray through want . . . He has been fighting since the days of Horus, never conquering nor yet being conquered. He never announces a day for fighting, like an outlaw thief of a gang. As I live! As long as I was around those bowmen were walled off . . . Don't give them a thought! The Asiatic is a crocodile on the riverbank: he snatches [people] on the lonely road, but he will never seize at the harbour of a populous city.' His words echo age-old complaints of settled rulers at the infuriating habits of nomads – furtive, demanding, impoverished, always on the make. And damned unsporting. Chaps don't even know the rules of war. Not to worry, though – Akhtoy's arrogance echoes that of another later empire:

> Whatever happens we have got
> Hieroglyphs, and they have not.

The fact of the matter was that Akhtoy's arrogance was somewhat fragile. Beset by Asiatics, he was not much of a master in his own house. His writ did not seem to run to the Lebanese coast, let alone to the hinterland of 'Asia'. It took a stronger man, Mentuhotep, based in Thebes, to secure his dynasty, the 11th, and begin the task of reuniting the country. Armies numbering in thousands criss-crossed the Nile Valley, with Thebes, the centre of resistance and national revival, desperate to regain control of its desert approaches. It must have been quite a struggle. One Nubian general, Tjauti, left his mark in a part of the road beyond the Wadi el-Hol, claiming he made the road to secure the desert crossing after the 11th Dynasty Theban ruler, Antef, had blocked it (an earlier Antef than the temple-builder). This Antef apparently retaliated: another graffito refers to the 'strike force of Antef'.

Clearly, many of the Wadi el-Hol remains date from this period, the Middle Kingdom (roughly 2140–1785 BC), when the nation was reformed. One of the inscriptions in the Wadi el-Hol records the journey of an official on his way from Abydos to Thebes for the funeral rites of Mentuhotep around 2010 BC. But such details are rare. This is a shadowy time, with little extant to reveal what happened. Apparently, it took a while to re-form a country that had disintegrated, perhaps because it was devastated during a civil war by unemployed mercenaries, among them Asiatics. Inscriptions mention overgrown ruins, silted-up wells, blocked canals, until a renaissance under the first 12th Dynasty king, Amenemhet I (Ammenemes, as the Greeks called him). He described how he seized power in dramatic, if uninformative terms: 'I stood on the limits of the land and surveyed its interior. I curbed lions and caught crocodiles . . . I made the Asiatics do the "dogwalk",' which sounds like a suitably subservient gait, whatever it meant. His son, co-ruler and successor, Senusret, promised to reassert central rule south, building a temple in Thebes and re-establishing royal authority to Elephantine, the town on an island in the Nile near the Nubian border. As Sinuhe says of his master Senusret (Sesostris in Greek), 'his joy is to plunder barbarians . . . He was begotten to strike Syrians, and trample sand-farers.' Once again, 'Asia' was up for exploitation, both by force and diplomacy. An inscription published in 1980 speaks of an army sent to the turquoise mines in Sinai and to the Lebanese coast returning with booty and 1554 Asiatic prisoners.

Indeed, Sinuhe, on his way to Retenu (northern Palestine), paints a dire portrait of the 'Asiatic' lands beyond Egypt's reach. Wherever he goes, he finds mere nomads pasturing flocks and raiding each other and obsessed with pasturage and wells. There is some subsistence farming, but most people hunt. Away from the coasts, there are no rich towns, only feuding clans. This was the back of beyond. No true Egyptian belonged there. Sinuhe was the beneficiary of royal largesse – 'like any ruler of a country' – when he was summoned home. His story contains a clear subtext: Egypt is safe again! Come home, you exiles, to your patient, understanding and forgiving king!

The Road of Horses, as it would later be known, came into its own again a couple of centuries after the probable date of the Wadi el-Hol remains, when Egypt was again torn apart by two catastrophes. Southern Egypt fell into the hands of an obscure Nubian kingdom, while the north was taken over by foreigners known as Hyksos, operating from their great capital in the eastern Delta, Tel el-Daba (also known as Avaris). In the words of the third-century BC historian, Manetho, 'For what cause I know not, a blast of God smote us; and unexpectedly from the regions of the East, invaders of obscure race marched in confidence of victory against our land.' The identity of the Hyksos is somewhat less obscure than it was: indeed, the word Manetho uses is better translated as 'vile' – the same term as used by Akhtoy – a common way of describing foreigners. Possibly there was no invasion, but simply a takeover by resident Asiatics who, it seemed, looked for guidance or alliances to the 'princes of Retenu' in northern Palestine. From their names, they too seem to have spoken a West Semitic language, something related to ancient Hebrew. It took another century for the Theban rulers to drive out these barbarians.

Within this time and these events lived the Asiatics responsible for the Wadi el-Hol alphabetical graffiti.

Assume, along with John Darnell, that they are living in Egypt around 2000 BC. Imagine a population that shared traits with many different sorts of expatriate communities. Some, like Jews in nineteenth-century Europe, came to trade, and remained, steering a tricky line between tolerance and disdain. Others came as impoverished outcasts to find work of any kind. Thousands were in private service: in a 13th-Dynasty court case recorded on papyrus, one wealthy Theban landowner lists his 95 servants, 45 with names of Asiatic origin. Thousands more were there as prisoners-of-war, and were used as slaves on government service, building dams, temples, roads. All were mere Asiatics to the supercilious Egyptians, for all spoke related West Semitic languages, but amongst themselves there were hierarchies of status, from slave to officer to high official, and an allegiance to many different homelands. To each other, they must have been as different as African slaves in the American colonies, some so long established they had forgotten their roots, some with families back in today's Syria, Lebanon, Israel and Jordan.

But like early twentieth-century immigrants in America, they shared a common experience in their foreign land. Some were literate. A papyrus now in Berlin mentions a man referred to as a 'scribe of the Asiatics'. Like the Jews of the diaspora, the 'Asiatics' would surely have been smart enough to see that there was little use trying to rival the Egyptian establishment on its own terms. The Egyptian priestly and literary elites were probably as tight as medieval guilds, protective of their own authority, suspicious of anyone trying to muscle in. It took years to master the complexities of hieroglyphic, which was how they liked it. Script, status, power, identity: the four were indissoluble. If that were true for Egyptians, it would surely be true for any other culture that could master writing, as an ambitious 'Asiatic' would have realized. But how to abstract from their masters what was most effective without seeming to be a threat?

Anyone with some knowledge of hieroglyphic would have known that the script had signs for sounds that were shorter than syllables, for single noises that were common to Semitic and Egyptian. In hieroglyphic, there were 24–28 of these signs, depending on the period, which made a perfectly serviceable alphabet, as thousands of schoolchildren discover every year on day trips to great museums. The Egyptians themselves made use of this alphabet when writing foreign names. There were already forms of these letters used in the more accessible, written form of hieroglyphic known as hieratic and it is this script, as Darnell proposes, that could have acted as more of an inspiration for an alphabet than the carvings or paintings of fully fledged hieroglyphic. 'Asiatics' – possibly a few scholars under the leadership of one expert – could have created their own literate subculture, adapting Egyptian signs for Semitic. One expert, the Israeli archaeologist and epigrapher Benjamin Sass, backs this suggestion by pointing to the scale of the Hyksos capital,

Tell el-Daba, which could easily have supported its own academy, and to the achievement of Hyksos scholars in copying one of Egypt's great mathematical treatises, the Rhind Papyrus, now in the British Museum. True, the Hyksos dynasty came well after the date Darnell proposes for Wadi el-Hol, but there is no reason to limit Asiatic scholarship to the Hyksos dynasty.

Imagine an Asiatic scribe in Egypt wondering how best to write his own Semitic language. He can speak Egyptian and write in both hieroglyphic and hieratic, which Egyptians write on bits of broken pottery and papyrus with reed pens. Many of the symbols, those that stand for syllables we now transcribe with two or three letters, are of no use, because Semitic doesn't have the same set of syllables. He sets aside the determinatives as well, because they cope with ambiguities only in Egyptian.

He is left with a core of Egyptian symbols on which he can draw. About twenty-six individual sounds have their own signs, easily remembered because they symbolize their initial sound, according to the principle of acrophony: *net* (water) became *n*, *mu* (owl) became *m*. What if he borrows that idea? Not these same signs, of course, because in Semitic acrophony would be lost, as it would in any other language: not much point in an English child muttering '*m* is for owl'. Besides, the Egyptian sounds don't all have counterparts in Semitic sounds. No, it's the idea he seizes on. He has the *sounds* of Semitic, he has a choice of ready-made *signs*, and he has the principle of acrophony to draw on. The '*n* for *net* (water)' becomes, by a neat coincidence, '*n* for *nahas* (snake)'. Moreover, once the idea is accepted, he can apply it to any other Egyptian sign, ignoring its original purpose. All he has to do is to choose suitable signs which, when given their Semitic names, provide a memorable link between sign and the sound with which they begin.

For a start, he selects images of two everyday objects, an ox and a house. In hieroglyphic and hieratic, an ox-head 𓄿 was a determinative defining the sort of meat to be used in rituals like funerary offerings, but for Semitic speakers it could be made to stand for its initial letter in Semitic, the glottal stop which is sometimes described as a 'coughed *ah*', or the sound Cockney (or 'Estuary English' as it has become) pronounces for the *tt* in 'bottle'. Later, it would change its pronunciation again, becoming our letter *a*, with numerous pronunciations, depending on language and context. This is the reverse of our alphabet-book rhymes: A is for 'archer'. In effect, our scribe specifies:

'Ox' (𓄿/*alep*) stands for the initial glottal stop, which will later become our *a*.

In Egyptian, the symbol for a reed-shelter ⌸ was a uniliteral *h*. It may well have begun the list of alphabetic signs – recognized as a group, but of no practical use – in which case it would have been natural for our scribe to take it over as an early letter. 'House' in Semitic was *bayit*, later contracted to *bet* or *beth*, in which form it is still familiar as part of names like Bethlehem (Bayit-lachmu, the house of the Canaanite god, Lachmu). In the process of transferring from Egyptian to Semitic, the sign acquires a new initial sound:

'Reed-shelter' or 'house' (⊓⊔/bayit) stands for *b*.

And so on, for 22 or so letters. One sound, one consonantal sign, in principle, all based on adapted hieroglyphs. Though not every ancient Hebrew letter can be traced back to a hieroglyphic root, the principle is clear.

The scribe does not use vowels. Vowels are discounted in many early writing systems because they can easily be seen as the noises made as one consonant glides into another, or merely a way of getting into or out of a consonant. Egyptians didn't have them at that time, so it never even occurs to our scribe that these noises should be included. That won't arise until Greeks, Hebrews and Arabs discover the lack and start to make it good in their own ways.

This lone scribe: could those first pre-Proto-Sinaitic letters have really been the work of one man? It is possible. The letters that would one day be inscribed in the Wadi el-Hol hang together as a coherent invention. It seems unlikely, given the sophistication of the surrounding society and the existence of the Egyptians' own alphabetical signs, that a new set would emerge a sign at a time, here and there, from the minds of different scribes. Perhaps a committee was involved, a council of scholarly Asiatics. But it wouldn't have taken them long, once they had the idea to work on, and they could have been under the direction of a chairman – perhaps the same genius who came up with the idea in the first place. We can never know, of course; but it's possible, because something similar happened 3500 years at the other end of Eurasia, the details of which I shall get to later.

I like to imagine that these literate Asiatics were aware they were inventing something revolutionary. They were making a statement: hieratic and hieroglyphic is for *them*; this is for *us*, a way for us to show we are not despised foreigners. With these few signs, incomprehensible to Egyptians, yet easy for those in the know, Asiatics could record their transactions and possessions and mark their presence and give their various peoples their own funerary inscriptions.

But they could not have suspected how revolutionary their invention would be – that it would not only act as a focus for a vital, emergent people, but would leap the bounds of culture and language and spread wherever ambitious fringe societies saw the benefits of a simple writing system.

Such an adaptation could hardly have been a threat to the Egyptian elites, because it would not have been considered 'proper' writing. Imagine the head-shaking, the knowing whispers: those Asiatics, they don't even know how to use determinatives! But they didn't need to, because they could start afresh with a virtually new system. Over time, many groups would have included ordinary merchants and soldiers who knew the signs well enough to scribble, scrape and carve on rocks during mining and military expeditions (and perhaps on bits of broken pottery and papyrus, long lost or still to be recovered).

Darnell finds support for this scenario from evidence for Asiatic mercenaries in the Nile delta around this period, and from a hieratic inscription he found in the Wadi el-Hol in June 1999. It mentions express couriers, and lists a number of officers or officials, including 'the general of the Asiatics' named Bebi. From the other names and the writing style, Darnell believes Bebi was living about 1800 BC. Under Bebi's command, he suggests, were Asiatic soldiers and their families employed to provide protection and maintain way-stations for messengers on the road to Abydos.

The prize of finding the roots of the alphabet may well be within Darnell's grasp, for he has the skills and the determination to make a strong case. He has unrivalled expertise in the crucial field of 'lapidary hieratic', the form of the letters used by stone-carvers when they were adapting their script from free-flowing forms on papyrus. But the prize will not be conceded easily. In this intensely competitive field, other Egyptologists and Semiticists will raise objections. Some will claim that the chain of evidence is still tenuous, that his dating is dependent on the accuracy of dating related hieratic script, and that hieratic script is notoriously shifty, varying from scribe to scribe, school to school, century to century, with additional pitfalls made by scribes imitating styles of earlier centuries. This will take years to run its course.

And the Wadi el-Hol graffiti have counterparts, remember, in the Sinai desert. But before we venture there, it would be as well to understand what those Asiatics saw in an alphabet which they did not see in hieroglyphic. What, albeit unconsciously, were they aiming to do?

4

THE SEARCH FOR
THE PERFECT
ALPHABET

To the many millions who use it routinely, the alphabet seems the essence of simplicity, 'as easy as ABC'. But the sense of simplicity is deceptive, for the alphabet is a surface impression of hidden linguistic depths. Its few symbols are nothing compared to the complexity of sounds they represent, while those sounds merely hint at the complexity of language itself. The alphabet is simple as the street map of Manhattan is simple: not much use as a guide to the soul of the city. Our twenty-six letters form a lattice that gives a neat impression of control and understanding. Look deeper, and enter a morass that might have made our Asiatic scribe give up on the spot.

Remember how syllables seemed atomic at first sight? Under the microscope, they dissolve. How about words like *fire* (fi-er), or *meal* (mee-ul), or *schism* (ski-zum)? Are they one syllable or two? In fact, the syllable overlaps another unit of meaning known as a morpheme. Morphemes, which may or may not contribute to what we sense as a syllable, are the elements we nip and tuck to refine meaning, like prefixes and suffixes and other modifiers. Take a pair of sentences, *I'm happy my aunt has gone/You're unhappy your aunts are going*. Almost every element in those two 'simple' sentences changes according to the rules that are hard to bring to the conscious mind and extremely tedious to describe. *Un-* negates, *-ing* indicates an enduring act. You could say, 'You're happy your aunts aren't going,' but not that they're 'ungoing', though you could with a change of meaning and context call them 'outgoing'. Not that you will mean they are going out. Pronunciation shifts too, governed by hidden phonetic rules. The past tense *-ed* is a solid-looking morpheme, but it can sound *-id* (as in *spotted*), or a *-t* (*walked*), or a *-d* (*rolled*), depending on the preceding sounds.

Academic careers are founded on analyses like this, which appear like newly inflating universes from every phonetical and grammatical minutia. But to the unconscious they are child's play, literally. Even mistakes carry meaning effectively: *You'd better go, bettern't you*? In the

Parisian slang known as *verlan*, morphemes (or syllables – sometimes the two are hard to tell apart) are reversed, as in the name of this type of back-slang: *verlan* is *l'envers* (inverse) with its two main elements reversed. In other examples: *Vas-y* becomes *s'y-va*, *laisse tomber*/*laisse beton*, *n'importe*/*portenaou*, *mère*/*reum*, and *frère*/*reufre*.

With another increase in magnification, morphemes break into units of sound called phonemes. Phonemes are technically those sounds that help to signal differences in meaning in any language. One can form a morpheme, or a syllable (*I*, *a*); or it may take several. To alphabet users, some of these units are self-evident. *Pig* seems to be clearly made of three phonemes. Phoneticians prove it by substituting another sound for each unit in turn, and changing the meaning: *b*ig, p*e*n, pi*n*. Slips of tongue reveal that these units exist below the level of grammar, as when an announcer on a BBC French service, in a piece about South Africa, attempted a reference to '*la population immense du Cap*' and mentioned instead '*la copulation immense du Pape*'. Children delight in the Spoonerism 'fart smeller' for 'smart fellow'. Formalizing such substitutions reveals that English has about forty phonemes. These could theoretically combine into 1600 simple syllables, but in fact we use only about 300 (which would have to be the size of an English syllabary, if we had inherited our writing system from the Egyptians or Sumerians).

Have we reached rock bottom? Not a chance. The deeper you go into this analysis, the hazier the notion of phonemes becomes. In some languages, some sounds are perceived as the same (though they're not), and in some as different. Notoriously, Japanese find it almost impossible to distinguish between *l* and *r*, which can be a problem when discussing elections. The French confuse *ship* and *sheep*, while the English don't recognize a street (*rue*) from a wheel (*roue*) or a rather tricky sauce constituent (*roux*); the Germans cannot tell *bed* from *bad*; and in saying 'merry Mary's getting married' some Americans pronounce the stressed vowels all the same. In English, the *l* of *pool* is the 'same' as the *l* of *leaf*, though in fact it's not. In Russian and Polish, the sounds have different letters. The English commonly add an *s* to make a plural, which is an easy grammatical rule, but the sound varies: the *s* of *sets* hisses like a snake, the *s* of *stairs* buzzes. In *niece* and *tent*, the *e* sound is shorter than in *knees* and *tend*. The *k* sounds in *key* and *cool* are different (try it: the following vowels make you either grin or pout). German has two sorts of *u*, Swedish and Norwegian three, but they're not quite the same. To describe all these differences takes ten variables, and that's without taking stress and tone into account – when *telegraph* becomes *telegraphy*, the additional *-y* demands four other stress and tone changes.

These tip-of-the-iceberg subtleties in and between

languages support the conclusion that the alphabet does not do what it is supposed to do, namely provide a one-to-one correspondence between sign and sound.

To show how it doesn't, let me ask a strange question: does the alphabet exist? Of course it exists, you say! It is all around us, its letters are the ingredients of all that weight of written material that pours out of us every day, and of all the aethereal electronic writing that would be weighty if only it were printed out. But now zoom in, and see how the alphabet, like an object under a microscope, begins to dissipate.

Take one of the nice compact little signs, the eighteenth letter. Like all the others, it comes in two forms, *R* and *r*, to provide clues to grammar and context. So already it has a dual aspect. Actually, it has numerous other manifestations – dozens of ordinary typefaces, hundreds of odder ones, millions upon millions of minutely different handwritten variations. There are *r*s in typefaces yet to be invented, and in the handwritings of tomorrow's children. The variety is infinite. Yet among them, none of us would agree to have found the perfect, archetypical letter.

And that is just the written form. Could we agree on what the sign, which doesn't 'really' exist, represents? For me, it's the '*r*' sound in 'round the ragged rocks the ragged rascal ran'. My tongue is halfway back, towards the top of the mouth, and the sound can be made continuous, rather like the American '*ur*' in 'nurse.' But surely if it's a continuous sound, it must be a vowel? It is in Chinese, where it comes in several different tones, depending on meaning and dialect. In French, the *r* retains an element of vowel-ness, because the '*r*' in '*rue*' can be sounded continuously, as a sort of strangulated gargle. You can get close to the sound with the Scottish or German '*ch*,' (as in *loch* and *recht*), which is not the English '*ch*' of 'church.' On the other hand the German '*r*,' or rather the north German '*r*,' is, or may be, a uvular clatter that doesn't exist in English, unless it is in an imitation of a growl. But it's also OK in German to roll it off the tip of the tongue, as the Italians do. Not to mention all the childish renditions of the above, including the '*r*' that comes out as a '*w*' in English, as in 'wound the wagged wocks'.

Where in all this is the true '*r*' sound and sign? The closer you look the more it isn't there. It begins to look as if this ephemeral entity is rather less than the complete answer that is claimed. And the same is true of every single sound and letter, and thus of the alphabet as a whole. You are led to the ridiculous conclusion that there is no alphabet. The whole thing is an illusion.

Something is obviously wrong with this argument. It is this: the alphabet is an intellectual device with which to symbolize speech, and it is a mistake to equate it exactly with anything in the real world. Since it exists in minds, any physical representation is only one of an infinite variety. There is no Absolute Alphabet. The qualities of its existence are shared with countless other concepts, like Hamlet (was there ever, could there ever be, an ideal Hamlet?), or numbers. All numbers are abstractions: in the real world, '3' only exists as 3 *somethings*. The concept of '3' is a generalization from all groups of three objects, and as a symbol exists, like the whole edifice of mathematics, as a mental construct, part of the internal world we build to map the real one.

English is notoriously inept at representing this mental construct. *C* sometimes sounds like *k*, sometimes like *s*. *Qu* sounds like *kw*. *X* can sound like *gz* (exact) or *ks* or *cks* (but they're not the same in meaning, as in *tax/tacks*). *Y* can sound like *ie* (fly), or *i* (baby), or *ee* (yes). A sound that has no letter, the *s* in *pleasure*, transliterates as *zh* in *Zhirinovsky* and can also be spelled with *z* (azure) or *ge* (camouflage), though in other instances of *ge* you have to add a *d*-sound (rage, age). There are no less than 11 ways of spelling the sound usually represented by *sh* (na*ti*on, *sh*oe, *s*ugar, man*si*on, mi*ssi*on, suspi*ci*on, o*ce*an, con*sci*ous, *ch*aperon, *sch*ist, fu*chs*ia) and 13 if you add a local version of nau*se*ous and that odd interjection, *psh*aw. Oddities like this show that written English is, in part, a syllabary – you have to recognize the syllable in context to pronounce it correctly. George Bernard Shaw famously made fun of our infuriating orthography by pointing out that if you take the *gh* of *rough*, the *o* of *women*, and the *ti* of *nation*, you can spell *fish* as *ghoti*. Which, by the same argument, could make him George Bernard Pshaw, or Sure, or Shore, or even Tiough (na*tion* + th*ough*t).

Speaking of *ough*, as a certain T.S.W. did in a letter to
The Sunday Times in January 1965:

> I take it you already know
> Of *tough* and *bough* and *cough* and *dough*?
> Others may stumble, but not you,
> On *hiccough*, *thorough*, *laugh* and *through*.
> Well done! And now you wish perhaps,
> To learn of less familiar traps?
> Beware of *heard*, a dreadful word,
> That looks like *beard* and sounds like *bird*,
> And *dead*: it's said like *bed*, not *bead* –
> For goodness' sake don't call it *deed*!
> Watch out for *meat* and *great* and *threat*
> (They rhyme with *suite* and *straight* and *debt*),
> A *moth* is not a *moth* in *mother*,
> Nor *both* in *bother*, *broth* in *brother*,
> And *here* is not a match for *there*
> Nor *dear* and *fear* for *bear* and *pear*,
> And then there's *dose* and *rose* and *lose* –
> Just look them up – and *goose* and *choose*,
> And *cork* and *work*, and *card* and *ward*,
> And *font* and *front*, and *word* and *sword*,
> And *do* and *go*, and *thwart* and *cart* –
> Come, come, I've hardly made a start!
> A dreadful language? Man alive!
> I'd mastered it when I was five!

And what of other alphabets? How well do they represent the sounds made by their speakers? Russian isn't bad, because they had the benefit of a revolution. German is excellent, mainly because it is highly consonantal, and consonants are linguistic anchors. French, with its free-flowing vowels, is an orthographic disaster, though not as bad as English. What can outsiders do but despair with at least eight different ways of spelling the sound that in English doesn't exist, the short front *e* that can be spelled *é* (*été*), *ai* (*j'ai*), *ais* (*mais*), *ait* (*il était*), *aient* (*ils étaient*), *è* (*évènement*, though, just to confuse us, the second *e* can also be with an acute), and *et* (*jet*). OK, there are distinctions, but they're hard for non-French speakers to hear.

By the mid-nineteenth century, the mismatch between sound and symbol had long been obvious to linguists, who determined to pin down language on the printed page. Isaac Pitman, the inventor of the most successful shorthand system, devised no less than seventy-two phonetic alphabets and founded a 'Fonetik Soseieti' to promote his schemes. Others followed, of increasing complexity. In 1886, leading phoneticians founded an association aiming to agree on a way to transcribe sounds, devising a system that became the International Phonetic Alphabet (IPA). In 1905, the association gained a new member, Daniel Jones, a postgraduate in phonetics, who started to teach language studies at University College, London, two years later. Over the next twenty years, Jones established the first British phonetics department, turning it into the most famous in the world. Largely as a result of his work, the IPA won international acceptance. Its aim was to extend the scope of the alphabet itself: to provide a separate symbol for each 'meaningful' sound in all the world's languages. The system, which undergoes steady revision as research extends the range, at present contains over 170 symbols – 74 consonants, 24 vowels, 31 diacritics (accents), a dozen tone indicators, a dozen stress markers, and 18 extra symbols for rarities like the epiglottal plosive. Sub-specialists have yet more symbols to record speech disorders, and habits like whispering or talking through the nose, even imitating Donald Duck.

Phonetics had something of an image problem, until the recent need for voice synthesis increased its appeal. But there was a time, a century or so ago, when the new science seemed on the verge of achieving the holy grail of linguistic analysis: a sign for every sound in every language on earth. Some foresaw dramatic consequences. Foremost among these was George Bernard Shaw, socialist, polemicist, the greatest playwright of his day, who thought that phonetics should become a key to social advancement by ironing out that great pillar of the English class system: accent. It would do so, needless to say, by levelling upwards, turning working class into middle class. In 1912, he began work on *Pygmalion*, the play which brought this arcane subject into the limelight.

It seems an odd title today, but a century ago theatre-goers were familiar with the mythical Greek sculptor who fell in love with his own creation. In this wonder of comedy, satire and fairy-tale, Pygmalion the sculptor becomes Professor Henry Higgins, phonetician, who creates from the raw clay of the streetwise Eliza rather more than he intends – an upper middle-class lady who is also a self-assertive young woman. The musical version, on stage and screen, brought the story to millions.

Where did Shaw get this material? Shaw had met Britain's most famous phonetician, Henry Sweet, whose reputation for brilliance was won despite a fourth-class degree that barred him from any high academic post. His *Handbook of Phonetics* (1877) had made English and London world leaders in this new science. In his masterly summary of the subject in the classic 1911 edition of the *Encyclopaedia Britannica* (just before his death as a mere 'Reader' at Oxford) Sweet stated the potential benefits of phonetics, views that paralleled – perhaps even inspired – Shaw's: 'It is only by the help of phonetics that it is possible to deal effectively with vulgarisms and provincialisms of pronunciation and secure uniformity of speech.' The article also argues that another purpose of phonetics is to reform spelling in all languages – an issue close to Shaw's heart, and a cause taken up by the Simplified Spelling Society, founded in 1908.

Shaw himself said in his introduction to *Pygmalion* that 'there were touches of Sweet' in Higgins, claiming also that he owed more to the Poet Laureate, Robert Bridges, and knew no other phoneticians at all. In this, he was being somewhat economical with the truth. He knew Bridges was no phonetician, and he had in fact based Higgins's academic work on that of Daniel Jones. Eliza's vowel training was Jonesian, as was the phonograph, larnygoscope, burners, tuning-forks, organ pipes with bellows and other equipment specified in the stage directions. Jones later told a former student how Shaw came by the name of his hero: 'It was whilst riding on the deck of a bus through south London, wondering what name he should give him, that he saw over a shop "Jones and Higgins". As because of the fiction, "he could not call me Jones, he called me Higgins".' Shaw even offered to give Jones complementary tickets to the play in perpetuity. The acquaintance continued. Later, in the 1920s, Shaw took an American actress named Molly Tompkins in hand and determined to iron out her American accent. He sent her to Jones. 'You still have very queer Rs from the cockney standpoint,' he wrote to her. 'Don't pick up smart English, which is bad English: all you need to do is drop certain provincialisms.' The two later worked together in the BBC's Pronunciation Advisory Committee, and in 1946 Jones, accompanied by James Pitman, MP and grandson of Isaac 'Shorthand' Pitman, went to see the aged Shaw to make a plea that the great man should benefit the Simplified Spelling Society in his will. Shaw gave them short shrift, never even offering them a cup of tea, and left much of his vast estate to finance work on his own entirely impractical alphabet.

So why did Shaw not acknowledge Jones? After all, the characters of Higgins and Jones were so different there was no chance of confusing them. Higgins is boorish, cantankerous, irascible, and a fine stage presence. Jones was uncharismatic, the very image of the academic: mild-mannered, slight of build, precise, totally devoted to his subject throughout his long life (he died in 1967). He had no small-talk at all. One student recalled his first meeting: 'Jones answered the door himself, let me in, and said "How do you do? Come in and sit down. Would you please say a voiced bilabial implosive?" '

Probably the link was kept secret because both men knew Shaw's purpose was artistic, not scientific. Jones, on the point of being made a professor, with an expanding department in a new and uncertain science, was not keen on the sort of publicity Shaw would bring. He went to the first night of *Pygmalion* on 11 April 1914, and was appalled. Here was a very English expert in phonetics, of which in real life there was but one, dallying with a beautiful working-class girl who was also his pupil, and who used language deliberately designed to affront middle-class hypocrisy: 'Not *bloody* likely!' No wonder Jones wanted the link kept quiet. Shaw took his point, and used his Preface to mislead. Both were men of their word. Phonetics retreated to its academic backwater.

Still, *Pygmalion* contributed to a popular notion that it was possible, in theory, to record the sounds of human speech in signs. It isn't. The IPA, though employing almost ten times as many symbols as the alphabet, is highly selective. It has to be, because the range of noises humans can utter when speaking forms a spectrum that can be divided infinitely. The IPA symbols are little more than a hint of the full range of possible sounds. It is this variety that makes phonetics so fascinating to its students and so tediously technical to outsiders. Some sounds are common to most languages, some are rare. Welsh speakers often claim that they are unique in possessing a lateral fricative, the slushy *ll* of *Llanelli*. Actually, Zulu has it as well, in both voiced and unvoiced forms. And so does Mongol. A Welsh speaker would have no trouble in pronouncing the *l* in the Mongol capital Ulaanbaatar. The click sounds of southern African languages (they are found only in southern Africa) are the subject of a whole book (by J. W. Snyman). John Wells, Jones's second successor as Professor of Phonetics at University College, London, has gone so deeply into the various pronunciations of the letter *r* that he had to coin a word for his sub-speciality: 'rhotics', which now has its own list of specialist publications.

These subtleties are of no concern at all to most of us, who simply speak without analysing how we do it, but they do matter to the many thousands who sing in choirs, and especially their conductors. If, for example, you are conducting the *Hallelujah Chorus*, you run into problems instantly. Is it 'Hallel-u-jah', following the Hebrew for 'Praise ye Jah(ova)' or an Anglicized 'Hally-loo-yah'? When your choir comes to diphthongs and consonants, there are harder decisions to make. Take the word 'Christ', especially if held on a long note: the word breaks down into phonemes that slide into each other: *k-r-ah-ee-s-t* which have to fit into (say) the four beats of a semibreve. Do you hold the '*kra-a-a-h* . . .' and end with a quick '. . . *ee-st*'? Or encourage everyone to sing a minim '*kra-a-h* . . .' and another minim '. . . *e* . . .' and then a sudden '*st*'? Or some smoothed-out diphthong with one sound merging into the next, before the final '*-st*'? Is the *-st* just off beat, or part of the last beat? There are no right answers. Conductors have to make their own decisions and impose them, as part of the process of creating a unified sound.

Pure sounds may exist for seconds in music, but in speech no sound stays 'pure' for more than milliseconds, unless uttered in special laboratory conditions, as Eliza Doolittle does, for example. Some sounds are 'pure', in that they are the same backwards as forwards, like the extended '*a-a-ah*' requested by doctors when viewing throats. But some, like *p*, are actually composites with their own narrative structure: silence, a gathering of muscular forces – lips, lungs, air pressure – then a release of air, an opening of the lips and an engagement of the voice-box. You could no more say it backwards than unburst a balloon. In speech, any sound is affected in subtle ways by what precedes and what follows, and by tone, emphasis or the position of the tongue, which may or may not bring in the nose as part of the sound chamber. The attempt to understand exactly what goes on has linked phoneticians with a new breed of scientist, the speech synthesizers. Nowadays, those who aim to synthesise speech focus not on the 'pure' sounds, but on the ways sounds flow into each other in so-called diphones. Only when the right choice is made of the three hundred or so possible combinations does machine-synthesized speech become comprehensible. And merely choosing correctly does not produce a natural-sounding voice: witness the robotic tones of Stephen Hawking's synthesizer. For naturalness, the synthesizer must glide from sound to sound.

And the sounds are only part of the problem. To choose the right sound from several possibilities, a computer has to recognize context. It may use the same rule to say *am* and *ham*, but it will need other, higher-level rules to modify the *ham* element in *shame* and *Thames*. Diphones have to be overlapped, then have the transitions smoothed out by a phonetic paintbox. Many theoreticians argue that this can only happen when a synthesizer understands what it is saying, which implies an artificial intelligence beyond anything yet achieved.

The purpose of this discussion of several different specialities is to re-emphasize that the often-stated aim of the alphabet to represent every sound by a single sign is a myth. It is not uniquely efficient, as used to be claimed, at least not in the sense of a one-to-one match between sound and sign. The plosives (*p, t, k*) cannot exist without their explosion into a vowel, so that they are either a 'silent sound' or a syllable. The alphabet is at best a distillation, at worst a highly complex corruption, of speech, and no alphabet could ever be much of a guide. Even the IPA, which has the advantage of being international, provides only the roughest of approximations, and it can only do so because it is of a size and complexity that exceeds that of a simple syllabary (like Japanese).

What, then, can an alphabet best achieve? Its hidden aim is very different from its stated one. Its purpose is to reconcile two antagonistic pulls: to have as many symbols as possible to represent its language as accurately as possible; and at the same time to restrict its symbols to ensure easy learning, easy writing and easy reading. It is self-evidently impossible – any child can recall, use and play with hundreds of sounds, but few adults can match meaning to that many sounds in shape-form. On the other hand, too much simplicity leads to ambiguity. Suppose, for example, you simplify a nursery rhyme by omitting the vowels, in a condensed pseudo-Semitic version:

JCKNDJLLWNTPTHHLL

It's hard to get. Comprehension is aided by breaking it into words and a couplet:

JCK ND JLL
WNT P TH HLL

It's still ambiguous to those not raised with nursery rhymes, because vowels can be added any which way:

Jockey nod Jolly

Won't ape thy holly.

Better to add the vowels and live with the additional complexity. It seems that the best way of balancing the conflict between ambiguity and overload is to create a system of between twenty and forty signs, and make the best of the mismatch between symbols and sounds.

And then the alphabet comes into its own, as a highly abstracted impression of language whose weakness becomes a strength. It is precisely because it avoids the complexities of the IPA and syllabaries that it works, allowing for the flexibility, the fuzziness, the rough and ready fit between symbol and reality that is the essence of language itself.

The fuzziness of English orthography should be especially celebrated – it's the written counterpart of a language that forgives being spoken 'badly', and thus wins such widespread popularity.

The perfect alphabet may be a hopelessly remote ideal, but it is possible to do a better job than history has made of the western alphabet, in any of its manifestations. We know this because there is an alphabet that is about as far along the road towards perfection as any alphabet is likely to get. Emerging in Korea in the mid-fifteenth century, it has the status among language scholars normally reserved for classic works of art. In its simplicity, efficiency and elegance, this alphabet is alphabet's epitome, a star among alphabets, a national treasure for Koreans and 'one of the great intellectual achievements of humankind', in the judgement of the British linguist, Geoffrey Sampson. It's a story worth telling, because it shows to what heights the alphabet can be taken, and its limitations.

Since Korea became a unified nation around AD 700, it evolved into a sophisticated and assertive society, though always in the shadow of its big brother, China. Chinese culture, trade, literature and language permeated Korean life. Yet it was not a happy match. Korean society did not mirror Chinese, nor did its language fit easily with Chinese script. The two belong to different language groups: where Chinese builds sentences of small words, Korean adds suffixes to modify roots. For adapting Chinese script, Koreans employed a complex system of transliteration (*idu*) that used some Chinese symbols for their meaning and others that sounded vaguely like Korean. Whichever system was used – Chinese by the upper classes or *idu*, which was supposedly for ordinary people – writing was inefficient for a society proud of its learning and book production. Like China, medieval Korea printed with both woodblock presses and movable wooden type, even metal type: Korea was the first country in the world to use movable metal type, in a work entitled *Prescribed Ritual Texts of the Past and Present*, printed in 1234.

In the early fifteenth century, a new dynasty, Choson, was emerging from the disorders that attended Korea's escape from Mongol-Chinese control in 1356, consolidating power through a rising class of scholarly bureaucrats. The fourth Choson king, Sejong, who came to the throne in 1418 at the age of twenty-two, was a remarkable character: scholarly, reform-minded and ambitious for his people, with a rare combination of determination and tolerance. He was a committed Neo-Confucian, a philosophy imported from China by his grandfather who had made it the new dynasty's official ideology. Sejong was a man with a vision of a world in which men lived in harmony with mankind, and mankind lived in harmony with nature. For Sejong, this was more than an ideal. He was that rarity among rulers, a man determined to do good, with the power to do it. Choosing specialist scholars from his own 'research institute', the Hall of Worthies, he reorganized ritual and protocol, equipped an observatory, revised the calendar, standardized weights and measures, set guidelines for the study of history and oversaw the syllabus of an interpreters' school. He made sure the work was published, encouraging the latest techniques: of the 308 books he produced, 114 were in movable metal type. In his thirty-two-year reign, he created the foundations of a dynasty that lasted five hundred years. With good reason, he is now regarded as Korea's best and brightest monarch.

Sejong became increasingly concerned that his good works were not available to ordinary people. What use was it to have Korean folksongs collected or agricultural handbooks published if the results were read only by scholars? His sense of frustration came to a point with the publication of a primer in Chinese on the Confucian virtues of piety, loyalty and wifely constancy. Convinced that people would do what was right if they only knew what it was, he urged teachers to get out into the countryside with it and 'gloss and repeat the text, even to women and girls'. But all the effort could be wasted: 'Since the common people generally do not know characters, even if this book is distributed, how can they know its meaning and act upon it?' Even if it was in *idu*, it wouldn't be much more accessible. There was only one thing for it: he would give his people their own new writing system.

This was an original and brave idea, because it would challenge the prestige and traditions of his own establishment, the Chinese-speaking scholar-bureaucrats he would need to introduce it. He would have to proceed carefully. Discreetly, promulgating no new law, Sejong commissioned a team headed by a great scholar, Sin Sukchu, who spoke Chinese, Mongol, Japanese and Jürchen (the language of the people on Korea's northern border). Tradition demanded a Chinese source, if possible. But in several research trips to China the team found no orthographic rules that they could re-apply to create a Korean script.

There was, however, inspiration in the former Chinese dynasty, that of the Mongols. To look to the Mongols for guidance was another bold choice, for the Mongols had devastated Korea two centuries earlier, their Yüan dynasty then seizing direct control of the north until driven out in 1356. But that was past. The important thing for Sejong was that Chingis Khan, father of the Mongol empire and its Mongol–Chinese dynasty, had introduced an alphabetic script from the Tukish-speaking Uighurs for the writing of Mongol before the conquest of China. Then his grandson, Khubilai, khan and emperor, had commissioned a new script from a Tibetan lama, Phags-pa, which was used to write the major languages of his domains – Chinese, Mongol, Tibetan, Turkish and Sanskrit. Both worked better than Chinese script for non-Chinese languages. So the new script had to be an alphabet. Sejong thus became the advocate of an idea the roots of which, as we now know and he didn't, extended back to those scribbles in the Wadi el-Hol some 3500 years before.

Sejong, now a middle-aged man suffering from diabetes, nervous disorders and eye complaints, immersed himself in his task, apparently carting notes around even on trips to the curative hot springs of Onyang and the Pepper Waters of Ch'ongju. His worried staff drafted a deferential letter: 'Are you going to work assiduously on this alone, thereby impinging on the time for convalescence and treatment?' Sejong took no notice.

In the winter of 1443–4, the twenty-eighth year of Sejong's rule, the great work emerged from its secretive gestation and was published as *The Correct Sounds for the Instruction of the People*. (In fact, to later historians, the alphabet's appearance came to seem like a divine revelation, because *The Correct Sounds* was lost for five hundred years, until its rediscovery in 1940.) Sejong's introduction (in Chinese) summarized his purpose in a classic statement which, in its Korean version, schoolchildren now learn by heart:

> The sounds of our language differ from those of China and are not easily conveyed in Chinese writing. In consequence, among the ignorant, there have been many who, having something to put into words, have in the end been unable to express their feelings. I have been distressed by this, and have newly designed a script of 28 letters, which I wish to have everyone practise at their ease and use to advantage in everyday life.

Sejong had no doubt about the benefits and the ease with which it could be learned.

> A wise man may acquaint himself with [the letters] before the morning is over. An ignorant man can

> learn them in the space of ten days . . . There is no
> usage not provided for, no direction in which they
> do not extend. Even the sound of the winds, the cry
> of the crane, the cackle of fowl and the barking of
> dogs – all may be written.

As he foresaw, his civil servants were appalled, voicing their
objections through a scholar, Ch'oe Malli. Only non-
Chinese barbarians like the Mongolians and Tibetans have
their own scripts, wrote Ch'oe. Does the king really expect
us 'to discard China and identify with the barbarians'?
What if this 'new oddity' catches on? 'The Culture of the
Right, which our country has amassed and accumulated,
will be swept from the earth.'

Sejong understood. He had no wish to confront and
delivered only a mild rebuttal. A new oddity? No such
thing. 'Since I have become old, I have made friends
with books of all kinds. I certainly did not make this
script simply because I was fed up with the old and
delighted with the new!' Besides, he had support enough
from scholars who saw sheer genius in their king's
alphabet. *The Correct Sounds* owes nothing to tradition,
one of them wrote in a concluding note to the king's
statement, for 'they have been perfected out of nature
itself . . . His Majesty is a godsend. His wisdom exceeds
that of 100 kings.'

This was not mere flattery. The judgement has stood
the test of time, for *Hangŭl* (Great Script), as it became

known, has several astonishingly original features. Its letters are based on an accurate analysis of Korean phonemes. It makes a clear distinction between consonants and vowels. Perhaps the most outstanding feature is that the shapes of the basic letters have significance (whereas the purpose of Roman shapes is lost in history). Sejong's letters are based on the position of the tongue when the sound is made: the *k* is a right-angle of the tongue as its base blocks the throat, while the *l* is the opposite right-angle (tip of tongue on front of palate). It also ingeniously refers back to Chinese practice, in that the letters combine into the 1096 Korean syllables which are written in blocks; but they can also be written separately, both horizontally and vertically, without loss of comprehensibility. In the words of its most expert western scholar, Gari Ledyard, 'there is nothing like it in all the long and varied history of writing'.

Rooted in practicality, *Hangŭl* also reflects Sejong's Neo-Confucianism. The whole alphabet divides into the two complementary opposites of *yin* – the female, passive, dark, dry and cold principles – and *yang* – the male, active, bright, wet and hot ones. The interplay of these two forces produce the five elements of wood, earth, fire, metal and water. In *Hangŭl*, the vowels are all elaborations on three basic Confucian symbols: a vertical for Man, a horizontal for Earth and a circle for Heaven. Moreover vowels are either 'bright' or 'dark', and consonants either 'hard' or 'soft', with further symbolic connections to the five elements depending on whether they are consonants of the back teeth, front teeth, tongue, lips or throat.

Yet, despite Sejong's authority and the beauty of his system, *Hangŭl* did not sweep away tradition. It found modest use in several of his pet projects, and in Buddhist literature, poetry and novels. The establishment refused to be convinced. Bureaucrats and scholars kept their precious Chinese for over four centuries. It wasn't until 1896 that the first newspaper was published in *Hangŭl*. But the system was forcibly suppressed under Japanese occupation between 1910 and 1945. After Korea's post-war division, North Korea committed to it, under its Communist dictator, Kim Ilsong. South Korea continued to hesitate, but *Hangŭl*'s popularity grew apace, as Sejong himself was adopted as an icon of nationalism, an image of human perfection, with his portrait on money, and streets and corporations named after him, a public holiday in his honour and a much-venerated tomb. In the 1990s, his great invention finally won.

Here, then, is about the best alphabet any language can hope for. Yet the best is not enough to win against the forces of conservatism. Sejong was caught by a paradox. His alphabet was the brilliant product of a highly sophisticated society. But to succeed it would have needed its society to be the exact opposite: a disadvantaged people with no conventions to reject.

Where there is no conservatism to inspire a drive towards perfection, however, something less than perfection will do. Bearing this in mind, we can return to the story of how an insignificant people rose to power, and what role their new script played in that rise.

5

INTO SINAI

Drive south down the Gulf of Suez. On your left the bone-dry mountains rise ever higher to Sinai's central plateau, guarded by jagged peaks that sometimes acquire snow-caps in winter. On your right is the Gulf of Suez, an impossible but appropriate turquoise. Somewhere ahead and inland, in the shadow of an immense cliff, lies St Catherine's Monastery, built in the sixth century on the place where, by tradition, Moses received the Ten Commandments. A few miles before the turning to the monastery is Abu Rudeis, a decrepit oil-company settlement. Here, turn left – if you have a 4 × 4 – drive 16 miles inland across flint-strewn foothills, and follow the Wadi Sidri for 15 miles. Leave the car, have a drink beneath one of the sparse acacia trees and start climbing up a steep path that leads up over barren rock. On the rock faces, you'll see carvings, and all around the remains of walls. Once, these were workshops and barracks. You have arrived at the turquoise mines of Serabit el-Khadem, the 'Heights of the Slave'. It was here, in these rugged and beautiful surroundings, that prisoners condemned to the ancient Egyptian equivalent of Siberian salt-mines hacked out the delicate sky-blue stones that were traded across the ancient world, and made marks of peculiar significance.

Egyptians and local tribesmen – just another bunch of Semitic 'Asiatics' in ancient Egyptian eyes – lived in these harsh mountains for millennia. Semitic legends peopled primordial Sinai, perhaps named for the ancient Chaldean moon god Sin, with aboriginal horites (mountain people), giants, barbarian Amalekites, or the cursed descendants of Esau. From early in the third millennium BC, the Egyptians started to send expeditions there, both to establish it as a buffer region and as a source of the turquoise worked by conscripted and enslaved Asiatics. For 1500 years, the mining expeditions came and went, in a rhythm that mirrored changing dynastic fortunes. A modest temple arose to Hathor, the goddess of turquoise, complete with sanctuaries, baths, porticoes and engraved pillars. These were abandoned when Egypt disintegrated in the so-called Intermediate Periods, first around 2175–2040 BC, again in 1750–1550 BC, and finally, and for ever, in about 1200 BC (with all the usual caveats about the inaccuracy of ancient Egyptian dating).

The British archaeologist, William Flinders Petrie
(1853–1941), was the first major researcher to come
here, in 1905. At the height of a long and distin-
guished career, much of it in Egypt, Petrie had already
developed meticulous techniques very different from
those of his contemporaries scrabbling for objects to
sell on the international art market. Speaking passable
Arabic, he was well prepared when he set out for Sinai,
where 'grim nature gives you the stone and the serpent
instead of the bread and fish'. His expedition of
thirty-four people was the largest to stay at the mines
since the Egyptians left 3000 years before (though he
was not the only outsider to come there. An eccentric
Englishman, a Major Macdonald, had lived in Serabit in
the mid-nineteenth century, trying to make a go of
turquoise-mining).

Petrie revelled in the adventure. One of his camel men
was the wily Khallil Itkheil, a 'picturesque rascal . . . who
could smile marvellously and show the whitest of teeth,
could dance to perfection, and look all the time capable
of cutting any man's throat'. It took their camel-train five
days to make the journey. They were there for three
months, living rough. The camels browsed on thorn and
tamarisk, the streams were fresh, their camel-men slept
out through frost and the occasional rain. Petrie loved it:
the high, dry air, the flow of talk (so different from that
'dreary and clumsy thing, the printed page'), freedom
from constraint in time and place, 'the absence of all

barrier or bound, the wide stretch of plain, the range upon range of hills'. Was this work? If so, it was also 'an intoxicating joy, one of the sweetest of pleasures'. It turned Petrie into a desert Wordsworth, an odd transformation for a man who was the very image of Victorian austerity.

First, he surveyed the mines and huts of Mughara, the Valley of Caves, where a rock-cut bas-relief of a pharaoh bashing a local chief into submission serves as a warning that Egypt would tolerate no foreign rule here. Eight miles beyond was Serabit, and its confusion of mine-holes and tumbled walls and leaning stelae. This was once quite a place: sanctuary, courtyard, temple, workshops and barracks combining to make a 200-foot building surrounded by a rampart of piled-up rock. All this was in the service of the sacred mineral, turquoise, and in honour of its goddess, Hathor, memorialized everywhere in rock-cut hieroglyphs and statues.

Then there were odd signs Petrie had never seen before, on eight stele-form 'tablets' cut into rock. He was puzzled. 'None of the inscriptions were intelligible as Egyptian, of any hieratic or debased type.' They were a definite system, but Petrie could only guess at the significance. 'I am disposed to see in this one of the many alphabets which were in use in the Mediterranean lands long before the fixed alphabet selected by the Phoenicians.' He suggested they were made by Israelites on their way from Egypt to the Promised Land.

These inscriptions suggested to the British archaeologist, Alan Gardiner, that the earliest alphabet was derived from hieroglyphic, a case he argued in a prescient article, *The Egyptian Origin of the Alphabet*, in 1916. In Sinai, he wrote, Egyptian meets Semitic. A series of pictures recurs several times: house, eye, ox goad, cross. One particularly clear sequence is on a little red sandstone sphinx, inscribed with both hieroglyphic and the local 'letters'. The hieroglyphs read: 'Beloved of Hathor, lady of turquoise.' Perhaps the statue was that gift to decipherers, a bilingual text. If so, and if the language was Semitic, then the letters:

could read b-^{c}-l-t, the supralinear^c being the Hebrew *ayin*, a harsh laryngeal sound absent in European languages, often missed out in transliteration. It could refer to Baalat, the female of Baal, a Semitic equivalent of the goddess Hathor. The link back to hieroglyphic seemed clear, from the house sign, adapted from hieroglyphic '*h*' as a '*b*' for *bayit*. Other inscriptions show the ox-head, both a common hieroglyph and the Semitic *alep*.

Together, Petrie's discovery and Gardiner's analysis inspired intense interest. In the 1920s and 1930s, dozens of books appeared on the origins of the alphabet, many inspired by the dream that these discoveries might prove the truth of the Bible. Five expeditions – four from the US, one from Finland – combed the area, and found more inscriptions. A leading US archaeologist, William Albright, doyen of orientalists and professor of Johns Hopkins University, gave the script its present name, Proto-Sinaitic, and said the language was West Semitic, or Canaanite. He thought he could identify twenty-three letters, with another four that remained enigmatic, and on this basis spun off into generalizations about grammar and vocabulary that later researchers regarded with scepticism. Various scholars provided unpersuasive translations of the words and phrases, the most extreme of all being a German, Herbert Grimme, who saw letters in every crack and colour difference. In one instance, he stretched forty-five dim and undecipherable squiggles into a deeply significant message: 'I am Hatshepsut, commander of the stone workers . . . It is fruitless! Give me life! . . . I am saved from my sins.'

Incidentally, by the time Petrie became terminally ill in Palestine in 1941, he was mentally as active as ever. Mortimer Wheeler, the eminent British archaeologist, saw Petrie as he was dying and marvelled at 'the immensity and impetus of a mind for which there were no trivialities in life and no respite'. Petrie, who was very well aware of his own mental abilities, wanted the world to understand the basis of his genius, and had left his head to the Royal College of Surgeons in London for research into his brain. His body was buried in Jerusalem's Protestant Cemetery; but, since the Mediterranean was a dangerous place at the time, his head, with the fine white locks and patriarchal white beard that made Petrie such an imposing figure, was kept in the hospital's laboratory until the war was over. In 1945 a head was shipped home, labelled as an 'antiquity'. Today, that head resides in the College's Hunterian Museum. The Israeli archaeologist, Benjamin Sass, the most thorough of modern researchers into Petrie's finds, became intrigued by this story. When hunting through old files in the Antiquities Department in Palestine, he noticed there was one missing. Perhaps it was the one that told the story of Petrie's head. But why was it missing? On a research trip to London, he mentioned this odd fact to Petrie's former secretary, Olga Tufnell, an eminent and stern lady. In Sass's words, 'I said I was interested in going to the College to check out the whereabouts of the head, "I forbid it," she said. So I didn't go.' Perhaps Olga Tufnell knew something, for the head in the museum does not have Petrie's glorious white hair. Several who knew Petrie, having been asked to identify the head, have come away uncertain. The mystery, which draws a steady stream of inquiries, awaits a resolution.

Sass was a newly qualified archaeologist when, in 1972, he was offered the job of deputy of the team responsible for antiquities in all Sinai, then under Israeli military occupation. Two days later he was in Serabit el-Khadem. Over the next five years he spent some three hundred days and nights amidst Serabit's austere and barren beauty, with its views across all central Sinai. It was a 25-minute walk up the steep footpath, carrying a 22lb pack, with water brought in from a well 3 miles away, but the hardships were nothing compared to the experience. He got to know every turquoise-bearing stratum, every inscription, every mine. It was the highlight of his life, in particular a moment in 1978 when he and a female colleague entered a shallow, out-of-the-way cave and saw two unrecorded inscriptions, a discovery that caused them to fall into each other's arms in delight. One of the inscriptions consists of four letters – *m-y-m-h* – containing the first proper *yod* (y) recorded in Proto-Sinaitic. In love with the site and his material, Sass realized there was no detailed survey of the inscriptions, and set about making one. The work became a thesis and then, in 1988, a book, which is the most authoritative account of these intriguing letters. It is hard to imagine it ever being superseded.

There are thirty-one inscriptions now recognized as Proto-Sinaitic, and another seventeen considered doubtful. Most seem to have been carved at the entrances to the mines, though some are now on loose rocks as the result of rock falls. Others are on statuettes. The four hundred or so letters are badly preserved, and don't in the end have enough links with hieroglyphic to form a bilingual key. Nine separate letters are unequivocal (B, H, L, M, N, Q, T and the two Hebrew glottal sounds, *aleph* and *ayin*), and another eight less clear, including Sass's *yod*. About twenty other odd signs and bits of grammar complete a flotsam that at present builds much of significance, but nothing of meaning. Some inscriptions are written vertically, some horizontally, but the direction in which they are to be read is unclear. Some letters are written now one way, then the other, in mirror images, as if the scribes were still unsure of the rules. Some letters suggest words: 'overseer of the miners', 'gift', 'eternity'. But in his erudite assessment of the inscriptions, Sass rejects earlier 'translations' as wishful thinking, except for Gardiner's 'Baalat', which is 'still the most important study done on these subjects'.

Dating remains as much of an issue as decipherment. Experts have stated theories and refuted each other for almost a century now, and still there is no firm conclusion, just ball-park estimates. Sass's best guess in the 1970s and 1980s was based on 'indirect and circumstantial evidence' suggested by the Egyptian system of writing foreign names, which was largely alphabetical during the late Middle Kingdom, about 1900 BC. Egyptian activity was at its height in Serabit around this time. But he is frank about the difficulties and remains willing to change his mind if better evidence emerges. 1900 BC seemed a reasonable date because he assumed the hieroglyphs and letters were contemporaneous. But they might not be. 'The inscriptions could also be from the time the Egyptians were *not* there,' he says, i.e. during the Second Intermediate Period, from 1650 to about 1550 BC.

We are left with another mystery, one concerning the authors of the script, but it is possible to speculate on the basis of the tenuous evidence. An Egyptian inscription from the reign of Ammenemes III mentions an 'Asiatic' royal called Hebded, the brother of an unnamed Prince of Retenu (Upper Palestine). The presence of a royal relative suggests that at least some of the Semites used by the Egyptians were not hapless prisoners at all but supervisors. That makes sense: one of the arguments against the theory that Semites developed the alphabet here was that prisoners would not have the time, energy or education to carve alphabetical graffiti. But as overseers they could have had all three, besides being bored out of their minds at being posted to this remote spot. In any event, the inscriptions are very few and rather amateurish, suggesting that the carvers were also few, perhaps members of a particular expedition. Perhaps the carvers had nothing much else to do but make their mark in rock, using the letters their forefathers had developed in Egypt a few years – a few decades? a century or two? – before.

At this point, our story reverts to an obscure group of Asiatics who were about to emerge, rather slowly, into prominence: the people we now know as Hebrews, founders of Israel, authors of some of the world's oldest works written in an alphabetic script. Their emergence, in particular the story of their escape from Egypt, is intimately tied up with the evolution of monotheism – and thus Judaism, Christianity and Islam – and of the alphabet.

It is the tricky relationship between myth and history in these three subjects – the Exodus, monotheism and alphabetical writing – that infuses the rest of this chapter. It could be that the evolution of the belief in a single god was dependent on an ability to record that belief and make it accessible; and that both recording and accessibility were dependent on the invention of the alphabet. In this view, god was not just the god of Israel; he was the god of the Alphabet. A sceptic may conclude that the Christian and Jewish god was invented because the technology had emerged to define this belief and implant it in its culture. A believer may say that god in his wisdom allowed himself to be revealed through this new mode of communication. Whatever the cause, it seems that both new god and new script worked together to forge a new nation and disseminate an idea that would change the world.

The usual question arises: when did this happen? The Bible identifies the events as historical truth, which should therefore be datable. Another school says the Exodus and its related events were a story told much later, as the Bible was written or edited into its present form. One thing is certain in this dispute between history and myth: the only available sources are the first five books of the Bible, whose familiar traditions were put into their present form centuries after the events they describe. Whatever theories arise, they must take that fact into account.

The origins of the Hebrews are much debated. From an early version of their name, *ebri*, some scholars relate them to a tribe, or sect, or group, or class known as Apiru, which originally seems to have been a term for 'outsiders' of any description, in particular cossack-style freebooters who roamed the wild borderlands of northern Canaan. Some, more obscurely, suggest that Hebrews were offshoots of the Shasu, also notorious marauders, who lived in and raided from their homeland east and south of the Dead Sea; they, like the Hebrews, seem to have revered the Hebrew god Yahweh.

In brief, the story told in the first five books of the Bible is as follows:

Abraham, presented in the text as the patriarch of the Hebrews and the father of the nation-to-be, whose own father came from Ur in Mesopotamia, arrives in the land of Canaan, where he adopts Canaanite beliefs, which includes a high god named El and his son, the storm-god Baal. His grandson Jacob begets twelve sons, later known as the founders of the twelve tribes of Israel, and moves the family to Egypt to escape famine. They are enslaved, yet prosper. Later, an unnamed pharaoh oppresses them, making them work in the 'treasure cities' of Pithom and Ramesses. A Hebrew child, Moses, is adopted by the Egyptian royal family, but becomes the saviour of his people. Committing himself and his people to a new god, Yahweh, he pleads for their release. Ten plagues reveal Yahweh's power. Pharaoh gives in, then renegues. With Moses at their head, the 'Children of Israel' flee from Egypt, across a sea which miraculously parts to let them through and then closes over the pursuing Egyptian army. Moses leads his people into the wilderness of Sinai, where over forty years he lays the foundations of Judaism. His successor, Joshua, leads his people on to nationhood in the 'promised land' of Canaan. Tribalism gives way to monarchy: Saul, David, then Solomon, who builds a great temple. Israel is founded.

For almost everyone with their roots in the Christian or Jewish worlds, the story is part of childhood, and has the clarity of historical truth on a par with other stories from history, like the American War of Independence or the death of Nelson. But historians who try to do more than simply retell the Bible story find endless problems in it, whether they accept the Exodus and Conquest as genuine, or reject both as myth, or try to steer some middle course. Counting by generations, which is the

Bible's only chronological guideline, gives a sequence that is all too often presented as fact: Abraham was born some time before 2100 BC, Jacob went to Egypt in 1926 BC, the Exodus started in 1496 BC, Joshua campaigned from 1456 BC, and Solomon dedicated the first temple in 1016 BC. All very cut and dried.

But this simply doesn't fit with Egyptian history or common sense. To take one discrepancy among many, the great 'treasure cities' mentioned in the Bible were not started until two centuries after the Biblical Exodus, if genealogies are used as a guide. Supposedly, the Exodus involved the 'borrowing' or 'appropriation' of much silver and gold from the strangely compliant Egyptians, followed by a mass migration of 600,000 men. Add women and children, and the number rises to – what? – one and a half million at the minimum, with 'flocks and herds and cattle'. This amounted to about 1–3% of the population of the *whole world* (about 50–140 million in 1000 BC, according to two wildly varying estimates). Then comes a pursuit by a vast army – how many troops would it take to retrieve one and a half million refugees? – and its cataclysmic destruction. Later, Joshua should have run smack into Egyptian regiments busy retaking Canaan for themselves. Yet the Bible does not mention any Egyptian armies there. Nomads straight from the desert supposedly seize massively fortified cities often invincible even to Egyptians, and then use iron at a time when they only had bronze.

And the Egyptian evidence of the Exodus, the years in the wilderness, and the Conquest? The archaeological evidence?

Absolutely none. No independent mention of a nation on the move, of a pursuit, of any cataclysm, of Israelite armies active in Canaan. No trace of a nation living in Sinai, let alone for the Biblical forty years, nor of destruction in the very cities supposedly ravaged by Joshua. Excavations in Jericho show no signs of walls from this time, let alone of them tumbling down, as they are said to have done at the blast of Israelite trumpets. (On the other hand, Jericho does sit on a major fault line, and has been damaged by earthquakes some thirty times.) Digs in the countryside have revealed no signs of warfare, only gradual settlement by pastoralists. The absence of evidence leads researchers in two directions: one opens the way to any amount of imaginative reconstruction; the other to radical deconstruction. Some historians suggest that Israel might have been forged on Palestinian soil, not in the wilderness at all; some that the whole story makes more sense if Solomon, for whose supposed glories archaeologists have found not a jot of evidence, is dropped as a historical character entirely.

To avoid such unorthodox thoughts, as the archaeologist and Egyptologist, Donald Redford, explains, some Biblical scholars have tried many ways to make sense of the mismatch between holy writ and harder evidence, imposing metaphors on numbers, squeezing timescales

133

here, allowing them full weight there. Nothing really works. In Redford's words, 'If the Biblical material in the Pentateuch, Joshua and Judges become a kind of smorgasbord of equally valid morsels of evidence, to be chosen or rejected at whim, we shall have about as many reconstructions of the premonarchic "history" of Israel as there are scholars willing to make the attempt.' It is hardly surprising that some scholars have dismissed the whole of the Exodus story as a myth.

Yet there is much to be explained. A people emerge to found a nation, which is perhaps in existence by the late thirteenth century BC. A seven-foot slab of engraved granite, found in Thebes a century ago, which dates from about 1208–1207 BC, the fifth year of the reign of Merneptah, states that Merneptah re-established Egyptian hegemony over a part of Canaan, during which 'Israel [the people] is laid waste' – the first non-Biblical mention of the Israelites (no hint, please note, that the ancestors of these same people had been Egyptian slaves not long before).* Certainly, Israel is in existence by the mid-ninth century, the time of the first independent evidence for a Biblical character, when King Mesha of Moab, a kingdom east of the Dead Sea, had a stele carved recording the defeat of his father by Omri, king of northern Israel. By

* Until the stele's discovery in 1896, it was widely assumed that Merneptah was the pharaoh of the Exodus. But obviously, if he defeated the Israelites, he couldn't be. Thus can one discovery recast 'history'.

then, Israel is well on its way to founding a new religion, with incalculable effects on later history.

What can be said about the roots of all this and of Hebrew writing? Nothing for certain, either for or against the Descent into Egypt, the Sojourn there, the Exodus or the Conquest. On inspection, every aspect dissipates into uncertainty and controversy. Since the story was put together centuries after the supposed events, it is almost impossible to unpick the strands of propaganda, oral folklore, literary tradition, varied authorship and history. Was there ever an Abraham? A Moses? In what sense did Israel exist between the first mention of its people in 1207 BC and its political emergence, presumably around 1000 BC? Is this story anything more than a fabrication designed to give a sense of identity to an emergent nation?

It's best to start with the writing of the story. The Israelites, having founded a nation, come to write their own history and explain to themselves their own success. The Pentateuch, the first five books of the Old Testament, was written in several stages, probably beginning some four hundred years after the events themselves, with additions and modifications continuing for another four hundred years until they were edited into their final form around 400 BC. At that time, Israelites were emerging from the catastrophe of the destruction of Jerusalem and two generations of exile in Babylon. It was a time for roots to be found and identity to be reasserted.

Much energy was expended in the nineteenth and twentieth centuries, mainly in Germany, in identifying different authors or editors, the main two being known as 'J', who supposedly wrote those sections which refer to god as Yahweh (*Jahwe* in German), and as 'E', who used the more formal 'Elohim'. Today, that scheme is seen as oversimplified, the Pentateuch being widely understood as a patchwork of oral and literary traditions cut and pasted together. Over these immense sweeps of time, each incident would have been simplified and dramatized and glossed to bring out the essential Jewish message: that the Israelites were god's chosen people heading under his guidance for a promised land. It is a story best told through a cast list of heroes and great deeds and turning points.

Let's propose a scenario for this great literary creation. Seeking the roots of their identity in events and people that mattered not a jot at the time, the editors gather ancient stories of what may have happened. They research sources, sketching and resketching, incorporating snippets of things that sound historical, which may or may not be factual, juggling places and times, until the narrative emerges in the most persuasive form. Perhaps they do on-the-spot research in Egypt, and draw a blank on their origins, because their ancestors were, after all, mere Asiatics, who had once had the gall as Hyksos to seize power, and whose memory had therefore been ruthlessly suppressed by the Egyptians, with the destruction of most of their monuments. The Hebrew researchers also find that in the capital, Tanis, the cult of Ramesses the Great endures. They connect the pharaoh who oppressed their ancestors with cities built under appropriate duress, Pithom and Ramesses (though they get the name wrong: the Egyptians called it Pi-Ramesses). They write in a part of their own legal system, according to which slaves are not released without means of support: hence the Egyptians' 'loan' of gold and silver. They know that the earlier pharaoh, Akhenaten, had a single god, clearly a statement of dominance, which, since they themselves have now been blessed with success, they readily adopt. They happily incorporate those tales in which their god helps them with miracles, thus displaying his superiority to other gods. They assume that the population in those far-off times was the same as that of their own eighth- to sixth-century Israel. Their ancestors' little escape becomes an epic. They write in a hero leader, who like all Asiatic cultures, looked to Egypt as the root both of civilization and of oppression. As for the actual amount of time that has elapsed since then, they haven't a clue, and have to do their best with genealogies. They place the origins of their slowly evolving faith in the tempering wilderness of Sinai and impose upon it a symbolic timescale because it makes the best story. They compress the emergence of their theology into a few dramatic episodes.

The problem can be focused by looking at the way their god, Yahweh, emerges, either from or into human consciousness, depending on your point of view. The issue of Yahweh's origins is a matter of endless debate. Yahweh in a later spelling becomes Jehovah. Both derive from the Hebrew spelling, the 'tetragrammaton' of consonants transcribed either YHWH or JHVH. In the earliest times, the Israelites still worshipped the Canaanites' high god, El. Indeed the very name of the tribe suggests as much: Isra-El, 'May El show his strength!' as it is in one interpretation. Since there is evidence that the Shasu god was named Yahweh, the Israelites possibly adopted the name from them, and the Bible's authors superimposed Yahweh on their history. There is some evidence for this in an eighth-century BC inscription found at a remote site in the Negev, Kuntillet Ajrud, in 1976. It speaks of 'Yahweh and his Ashera', a reference to a consort associated with El. Other inscriptions of the same period imply the existence of three different Yahwehs. This was several centuries after Yahweh had supposedly become a single god. Perhaps one day other inscriptions will mention children, for in Sass's words, 'what for would a deity have a wife if not to procreate?' It was as if those who worshipped Yahweh in the eighth century BC were still in the process of deciding exactly what his attributes were, a confusion reflected in the Bible. At one point, the Bible links Yahweh firmly with Moses, at another it backdates Yahweh's influence all the way to Abraham. These are discrepancies that did not seem to bother the biblical authors, who were happy to see Abraham, Isaac and Jacob as honorary 'Yahwists', much as Aristotle and Plato, Europe's intellectual ancestors, became honorary Christians to medieval scholars.

All this analysis makes the early biblical narrative look somewhat threadbare. But it's as well to remember that myths often conceal some sort of truth. It may be possible to sketch out a scenario that does not conflict with the accepted histories of Egypt and the rest of the Middle East, to impose another version of how it might have been. This version looks back with my own modern prejudices, which spice events with psychological profiling and circumstantial evidence. But remember as you read what follows that the biblical authors had the same idea: to create a convincing narrative.

Suppose Abraham and his descendants are personifications of Hebrew families that diffuse through Canaan and Egypt, forming part of the regular back-and-forth of traders, prisoners and workers, doing their best to make a living in alien lands. Some find work in Egypt. There they prove useful as workers, under their own overseers, some of whom marry into Egyptian families but retain a sense of their difference. Perhaps these Hebrews are comparable to the Jews in medieval Europe, preserving a precarious balance, despised as 'foreigners' yet tolerated for hard work, skills and intelligence. Some are indeed used as slaves, like other Asiatics – the authors of Exodus refer to the use of straw in Egyptian brick-making, a strengthening factor which was not used in Canaan.

There comes a point when some influential Hebrews see that their interests are best served by making a break and heading out of Egypt altogether. Normally, they wouldn't have much of a chance, for the eastern frontier is well patrolled, creating a sort of Iron Curtain that cannot be crossed without permission in either direction. It takes a specific order from on high to allow a mass exodus, hence the need for a leader, who we might as well call Moses, to beg pharaoh to 'let my people go', and the decision to escape only once pharaoh has changed his mind. For whatever reason, they go, either together or in dribs and drabs, in what the Egyptologist, Abraham Malamat, calls the 'Moses movement'.

When might this have started, assuming that some sort of exodus occurred? Some scholars have seen a window of opportunity in the reign of Ramesses II, an imperialist whose ambitions reached a sudden limit at the hands of the Hittites in the Battle of Kadesh, c. 1273 BC. Suddenly, Egypt seems vulnerable. All Canaan flares into revolt – an opportunity, perhaps, for a small, oppressed people to seize their chance. It took a decade to re-impose Egyptian rule. Another ten years later, the ageing Ramesses signed a treaty with the Hittites which opened a century of peace and prosperity. Ramesses II was also a dedicated builder of palaces, a sort of Egyptian Ceauşescu, and thus serves as the ideal oppressor of the future Israelites, forcing them into ever harsher servitude in his 'treasure cities'.

So assume no mass migration. But even a small exodus might have been a challenge to a local official, not pharaoh himself, but to someone who saw himself as a pharaoh's alter ego. There is a pursuit, not significant enough for mention in Egyptian official sources, but enough to sear itself into the communal memory of those who flee. It is not impossible. Slaves did escape sometimes. A letter by a military commander writing at the end of the thirteenth century BC – about the time of the first mention of Israelites on Merneptah's stele – describes such an incident in which he follows orders to pursue two slaves who escaped from Pi-Ramesses during the night and sneaked over the border into the wilderness of Sinai. Apparently, they got away. The officer instructs a frontier colleague: 'Write to me about all that has happened to them. Who found their tracks? Which watch found their tracks? What people are after them?'

There is one other possibility, suggested by a stele found at Elephantine, the Greek name for Yeb, Egypt's 'door to the south', which lies on an island opposite Aswan. Published in 1972, the stele's inscription records how, during the last years of Sethnakht II, in the 1180s BC, an anti-pharaoh faction bribed an unidentified group of Asiatics to help them in their revolt. The plot was

foiled, and the Asiatics driven out. It may be of significance that the plotters promised 'silver and gold', which
is what the Bible says the Israelites 'borrowed' from the
Egyptians. In the Bible, pharaoh knows the Israelites are
a force to be reckoned with, that in war they might 'join
our enemies and fight against us'. Hence the close
relationship with Asiatics, and its breakdown. Perhaps the
factional Asiatics were Hebrews who were involved in
civil war and were either expelled or chose to get out
while they could.

So now, some Hebrews, in whatever numbers, are on
the move. Perhaps a few hundred in strength, they take
their families and flocks through one of the shallow
papyrus marshes to the east of the Nile delta – a common
strategy for escaping slaves, to foil trackers and mire
pursuing chariots. There is no point taking the direct
route back to the Semitic lands to the north, the land
that future generations will designate as 'promised'. It's
not promised yet, because it's already occupied by local
tribes and the coast road is a regular highway for
Egyptian troops. Obviously, there's no going back. The
only alternative, as for other escapees, is a wilderness
existence in Sinai, living light, careful to leave no traces
for an Egyptian tracker (or a twenty-first century archaeologists, come to that).

Sinai as a whole, as much Semitic as Egyptian, formed
part of the no-man's land between Egypt and Assyria.
Imagine, over the centuries, a flow of traders and

soldiery, a major one along the coast and a minor one heading south and inland to Serabit. Once you were beyond the frontier, it was wilderness, a sort of Wild East, with Canaan – and scattered communities of fellow Hebrews – beckoning to the north.

To head into this rocky outback is a tough decision. The leader, our Moses figure, has to sell the idea to his people – people*s* in the plural, more likely, for this is probably an unruly bunch of fiercely independent clans. He needs them to stick together. Perhaps, like many other great leaders, he identifies with them so utterly that he sees them as a reflection of himself. He and his people are one. If this venture fails, it means more than failure: death, extinction, annihilation.

In the wilderness, something happens to him, something that many other political figures have experienced when in the wilderness, whether real or metaphorical. He acquires a sense of divine inspiration. He conceives the idea that he is under the direct guidance of a godhead. It would suit this scenario if Moses was historical, for we could portray him more firmly, drawing on his early experience as an Egyptian aristocrat. Raised an Egyptian, with a name that echoes the second element of Ramesses himself, he would have been familiar with the Egyptian god, Aten, the sun, whose worship as a unique deity was imposed by Ramesses' predecessor Akhenaten ('Pleasing to Aten'), as he called himself. But Moses' god obviously can't be the Egyptian god. It has to be his own god who speaks, whom he calls Yahweh.

Whatever name the Israelites called their god, however long the concept took to evolve, wherever it emerged, there are a number of things that in combination make Yahweh a brilliantly original conception, a conception that could only be sustained in writing.

Firstly, Yahweh, as he emerges in the Bible, is unrelated to a region. Actually, one Bible story presents this as an old idea. Before Jacob left Canaan, he had had a dream of climbing a ladder at the top of which he saw El, who made a promise that would have been extraordinary at a time when gods were strictly territorial: 'And behold I am with thee and will keep thee in all places whither thou goest.' But possibly this, like the name of Yahweh, was something that was imposed on the distant past. Anyway, by the time, this little tribe approaches Canaan, they are fixed on the idea that their god would be with them. This was an ideal god for nomads.

Secondly, this god is not (to start with) a god of temples and statues and officials and power structures and wealth. The idea that he was pure spirit came much later, but that ineffable quality has its roots in Jahweh's ban on 'graven images'. Again, this was an ideal god for a small group of dispossessed wanderers.

Thirdly, Moses establishes a direct relationship. His god speaks to him. Other gods had spoken to other high priests before, but never in these terms, for what Yahweh says is as revolutionary as his nature. No god had ever told mere mortals what to do in such direct and legally phrased words. These are not verbal obscurities, to be read and interpreted by acolytes, but commandments.

Fourthly, the commandments are part of a two-way relationship. Both Yahweh and the Hebrews live in challenging times, their existence threatened by other gods and other peoples. They need each other. In return for exclusive obedience and the abandonment of all other gods, Yahweh promises his exclusive support. His word was sealed in a contract, a Covenant, and kept under lock and key in the portable safe-deposit known as the Ark of the Covenant.

Finally, the laws apply to all Hebrews, high and low. The leader was now not like other kings, who placed themselves above the law because they made it (as Hammurabi, the great Assyrian law-maker, did). A law-maker may fall victim to those eager to write their own. But if the leader, too, is subject to the divine will, however demanding; if that law is literally hewn in stone; if he, as leader, is a model of obedience; then what else can believers do but follow? For the first time, might is not primary. Right – correct behaviour, morality – is the greatest good, to which physical power is subject (a somewhat limited morality, admittedly, since it applied only to the Hebrews). To a tribe of refugees threatened by a forbidding landscape, fleeing the battalions of an imperial power against whom they are as dust, this would have seemed an excellent survival strategy. With God and Virtue on their side, they had that most potent of offensive weapons: self-righteousness.

What emerges in the Sinai wilderness – or the meta-phorical wilderness – is a blueprint for group survival unprecedented in history (though not unmatched later, as we shall see). Machiavelli would have approved, for the Covenant provides divine sanction for a draconian and often brutal rule. Alien groups can be killed en masse, dissenters can be burned, rival cultists executed, as Elijah slaughtered the prophets of the old storm-god Baal.

As the future history of the Israelites shows, the blueprint worked, for a series of interconnected reasons:

- Their god was made in their image, and as they would wish to be: nomadic, warlike, dominant, bound by law and treaty.
- Law built on law, without the new undermining the old.
- The law became fixed – covenanted – because it was written.
- It was written because this band of desert people brought with them a simple script that was all their own: an alphabet.

Herein lay the key both to the leader's power and to communal survival – national survival, as it would become. This new god could not only make rules, he could make them stick, because, as the inscriptions at

Serabit el-Khadem show, it did not take a genius to inscribe them. Whether incised in rock, or scribbled on papyrus, or inked on to broken pottery, ordinary people could see right before their eyes the words of their god instructing them what to do, unchanging, from generation to generation. Never before had there been such a powerful tool for enforcing unity across time and space.

In all this speculation, I am arguing for a link between an emergent culture, a powerful leader, a new ideology, and literacy. Such a link may not have occurred before Moses, but it has occurred since.

In the lands north of the Gobi desert in the twelfth century, small tribes of semi-nomadic herdsmen had lived and fought together, exploiting the Central Asian grasslands for two millennia. Every now and then, clans had formed larger units, acquired kings, seized wealth from their sedentary Chinese neighbours and built empires, only to be blown away by rivals. Then a small group, the Borjigin clan of the Mongols, acquired a chief named Temujin, whose ambitions elevated him above petty rivalries. He united the feuding clans of Mongols and became their acknowledged leader. Renamed Chingis Khan, he turned on neighbours, welded them together, absorbed other neighbours, attacked China, turned west, seized most of western Asia and penetrated southern Russia, all of which laid the foundations for the greatest land empire in the world's history. Chingis's success was due in large measure to his extraordinary character. He was not merely a ruthless empire builder. He was also astute and flexible. When he was declared emperor in 1206, he realized that word of mouth was not sufficient to run an empire and a large army. That would take a revolution: clans broken up, a new power structure that gave him absolute authority, an army of almost 100,000 to be mobilized, booty itemized, laws enforced, blood feuds ended. All of this demanded effective administration, which needed records. He ordered his staff to adopt the script of the newly conquered Naiman tribe, who wrote using a system taken from the Uighurs, who inherited it from an Iranian culture, Sogdian, who had taken it over from Aramaic, who had it from old Hebrew: in effect, the script familiar to the Israelites 3000 years earlier. That same script remained the script of Mongolia until replaced by Cyrillic in 1942; but it is still used by those Mongols who live in China in the province of Inner Mongolia. It was until recently a key element in the Mongol sense of identity. Indeed, after the collapse of communism in 1989–92, there was a movement to reinstate it, until most conceded that the language had changed too much for a return. It would be like using Chaucer to record modern English. But its survival for seven hundred years is evidence that a new alphabetical script roots best in an ambitious young culture – young in this case defined by Chingis's own ambitions – with no other dominant tradition, and that the script is a vital component of a new sense of identity as tribe turns into kingdom and empire.

So we come full circle. The Israelites acquire a 'history' that encapsulates a grand truth: a small people once under the thumb of Egypt develop a new religion and grow into a nation.

Beyond this, however, it is hard to spot truth from fiction. In the scenario you have just read there is absolutely no way to tell whether the story is a poor record of contemporary events or made up later with suitably impressive historical details. In the current publishing term, it is a 'faction', a confusion of myth and history designed to make events and people live in the mind of the reader. If we look for facts, almost everything except the outcome – the emergence of the nation – is open. Perhaps there was no exodus and no Moses. Perhaps writing spread from the Hyksos capital, Tell el-Daba, not from a unified Egypt at all. If there was a flight from a pharaoh, perhaps it was small, or one of many exoduses.

In one sense it doesn't matter, because in this tale history in today's terms is subsidiary. Some things are right, and some wrong, and the whole thing is as true and as false as many another epic – the *Iliad*, the Norwegian sagas, the *Bhagavad Gita*, the *Nibelungenlied* – to the confusion of those who seek literal truth. It is a search without conclusion, for the Bible's history is deeply embedded in folklore *disguised* as history. You might just as well try to explain Shakespeare's *Macbeth* purely by delving into the history of eleventh-century Scotland. It rather misses the point.

Some things, however, must be literally true, because by the sixth century BC the Israelites were the living proof. At some point, their forefathers learned how to write in a consonantal alphabet. This is not to claim that these desert-dwelling Israelites were bookworms. Today, literacy is meant to be the birthright of all, without which no one can be truly part of society, but that is a recent attitude. Even in the Middle Ages reading was a skill possessed by the few. In ancient times and in small, tight-knit, semi-nomadic societies, literacy offered no great advantage except to those whose job it was to record and read. Consider the problems: to write anything, the writer had to get hold of a roll of papyrus or leather. Each record was a huge investment, in hardware and in time. If papyrus was used, it had to be imported from Egypt. If leather, it would have come from animals killed for meat or sacrifice, then washed, limed, scraped and stretched. Both were hard to write on. Scrolls had to be kept carefully, in a depository (hence the Ark). Reading brought another set of problems. Once carefully lifted out, the scroll had to be unrolled. That was hard to do. One papyrus roll in the British Museum is 133 feet long and contains 79 sheets pasted together. A scroll would therefore be used for several different purposes: it could have been 'visible song', to jog the memory of a bard or priest; it could have been a proof of power, a sort of sceptre which, in the case of the Israelites, actually contained the word of their god; it could have recorded legal transactions, to be checked if necessary, by a new office-holder, or the children seeking to confirm a dead father's actions. Whatever it was, a scroll was not like a paperback, to be carried around for enjoyment and convenience. Literacy was for the few. Even stone inscriptions were not always meant to be read, but to act as icons (rather as war memorials do today – the significance of the Vietnam Memorial in Washington is not only that it records individual names, but also acts as a sign that the nation as a whole remembers). Assyrian and Egyptian inscriptions usually included pictures to act as reminders of events and people; the writing itself may well do nothing else for the uninitiated but convey the feeling of power and inculcate fear.

Yet literacy as a private act was part of the culture by the eighth century BC. Anyone could use an old bit of broken pottery, known as an ostracon, to write on with a reed pen and ink made from the dust of charred wood. Ostraca were the scratch-pads of the ancient world, used for jotting down records, even writing letters, but often scribbled on and discarded. Some inscriptions seem to have been purely personal, an indication that literacy was indeed embedded in the culture. In a cave in the Judaean desert is a stalactite on which someone, a hermit-scholar perhaps, wrote a series of blessings, and a curse on anyone who removed his work, apparently with no public purpose in mind. In the eighth century, the townspeople of Jerusalem dug a tunnel linking a spring east of the city to the city's oldest area. An inscription marks the point at which the two parties of diggers met, describing the voices through the intervening rock becoming stronger as the rock face was hewn away. The words, which do not neatly fit the space made for them in a dark tunnel, seem to have been solely for the benefit of those doing the work. In a letter written on an ostracon in the sixth century, when Israelite culture was securely established, an officer replies to a superior who had apparently accused him of not understanding a previous communication. 'Your servant has been sick at heart ever since you sent that letter to your servant,' he writes, cut to the quick. 'In it my lord said, "Don't you know how to read a letter?" As Yahweh lives, no one has ever had to read *me* a letter! Moreover, when any letter comes to me and I have read it, I can repeat it down to the smallest detail.' Here is a man proud of his literacy, his memory and his oral skills. Is it too fanciful to imagine that wilderness dwellers had equivalent skills and pride half a millennium earlier?

The Bible's writers and editors made that assumption, perhaps on the basis of hard evidence. Their forefathers' first attempts at writing were as visible then as they are today, in the Wadi el-Hol and Serabit el-Khadem. It is not impossible that among the myths and partial histories being edited into the Old Testament in the eighth to sixth centuries BC was a folk memory of alphabetical writing, and that the editors fixed it in the most powerful image they could imagine, an image that no Egyptian or any other monument-building, stone-inscribing cultures could ever match: Yahweh descending to burn his laws in letters of volcanic fire into Sinai's living rock.

6

THE LAND OF
PURPLE

P erhaps knowledge of the alphabet filtered across 'Asia' during the time the Asiatic Hyksos ruled in Egypt (*c.* 1650–1550 BC); or perhaps it was the future Israelites who brought the alphabet from Egypt, some time after 2000 BC. Either way, it was not simply a real alphabet that spread, but also the *idea* of alphabet. The Israelites were not the only ambitious cultures on imperial borderlands, and not the only ones to respond to the emergent writing system. It so happened that around the middle of the second millennium there were numbers of likely communities along the coast of present-day Lebanon, Syria and Israel, living in ports like Byblos, Beirut, Sidon and Tyre. They, too, were Canaanites originally, now thriving away from their points of origin inland, but precariously placed between the three great land empires, Egypt to the south, Assyria to the east, and Khatte (the land of the Hittites) to the north. The coastal cities were on the shifting borderlands of Egypt and Khatte, influenced by both, in trade, religion and writing systems. Hieroglyphic reached north past present-day Beirut to Byblos, which around 1700 BC had its own form of Egyptian writing, while cuneiform spread south, into present-day Syria.

Bitter rivals, these city-states would not have united in self-defence, for they did not see themselves as forming a political unity, let alone a nation. They had no name for themselves. But they were united nevertheless, by a shared Canaanite ancestry, and thus by language, habits and writing. The Greeks called them Phoenicians, naming them for the purple dye (*phoinix* in Greek) for which they were famous. According to legend, Tyre's god Melqart was walking along the beach one day with his intended, the nymph Tyrus, when his dog bit a large sea-snail, a *murex*, that stained its mouth purple. Tyrus said she would only accept Melqart as her lover if he gave her a gown of the same colour. Melqart gathered up a handful of murex shells, used them to stain a dress, and won her.

Actually, his task would not have been quite that easy. Producing the dye is a lengthy process, which involves heating the snails in salt water for ten days until the hypobranchial gland oozes a nondescript yellowish liquid which turns purple in sun and air. The product is then boiled down to one-sixteenth of its volume. Since it took 60,000 snails to make half a pint of the colourfast dye, they were processed by the million for over 2000 years. The middens still hem in the ancient dyeing works. The process made a nauseating smell, so the works are all downwind of the town; in Tyre, which is an island, they put the works ashore. The dye cost the equivalent of about £20,000 for a small jar. No wonder that purple became a royal colour across the Mediterranean, and Phoenicians became rich.

Though there was no 'Phoenicia', only rival Phoenician ports, Phoenicians were loyal to one master: trade. They were the middlemen linking the great markets of Mesopotamia, the Hittites, Egypt, Cyprus, Crete and mainland Greece. With mountains to the east and great empires dominating inland areas, the Levantine ports looked seawards, seeking niches in trade patterns dominated by Egyptians to the south and the Minoans in Crete, and their successors the Mycenaean Greeks. These tough little city-states each had a king – more like a mayor, perhaps, except that the office was hereditary, which is a good enough definition of kingship. They complied when they had to, resisted when they could, rebuilt after enemy regiments left, and squabbled and made peace, all with remarkable vigour inspired by the rewards of survival. These port peoples needed a good writing system if only to keep trade records. Cuneiform or hieroglyphic both had their disadvantages, one being complexity, another being that time's whirligig brought new masters, new allies and exposure to rival systems. Hindsight reveals the ports to possess the two prime traits that made them ready for a new script: they were ambitious, and they were on the fringes of greater and more conservative cultures. They were ripe for the alphabet, knowledge of which was slowly filtering outwards from its southern Palestine dispersal centre.

In 1934, archaeologists excavated a tomb in Lachish, twenty miles south-west of Jerusalem, which from the pottery appeared to date from about 1750 BC. Among the remains was a bronze dagger, on which four 'letters' were scratched. Well, they may be letters. One of them looks like a Proto-Sinaitic '*n*'. Twenty-one other objects (daggers, tools, sherds, arrowheads and pots) inscribed with letters have since emerged in Israel and Lebanon from sites ranging from Qubur el-Walaida, near Beersheba, to Byblos, just north of Beirut. Their script is known as Proto-Canaanite, though Sass and others doubt if it deserves its independent status.

Perhaps the most intriguing find emerged in 1976 from a dig in Izbet Sartah, ten miles east of Tel Aviv. It is a bit of a pot, possibly dating from around 1300–1200 BC. After it was broken, someone who knew the letters that were spreading northwards used this fragment as an exercise tablet on which to practise his alphabet. This does not look like a school-child's hand, but nor is it the work of an expert. In five straggly lines of eighty letters, the would-be scholar tried a few letters several times, and missed out one (*mem/m*) entirely. The letters are written left-to-right, the opposite direction to that of later Hebrew, as if both possibilities were still in the air awaiting a final decision. Perhaps he was a jobbing stonemason who had picked up this new script on his travels, and spent a lunch break trying to remind himself of the full list and the order in which he had learned it. Or he may have had something more sinister in mind, and wished to fix his knowledge so that he could use it in an incantation, as medieval necromancers used the cabalistic spell based on the supposed magic power of the alphabet: abracadabra. Whatever his purpose, something seems to have clicked, because the fifth line is bolder, more confident. Perhaps there was a mate nearby to remind and encourage: come on, you've got room for one more, and this time get it right. Seventeen different letters stand out clearly, prefiguring most of the modern Hebrew alphabet, or 'abugida', to give it its technical term, with significant accuracy.

These objects, with their enigmatic little scrawls, are dated from about 1300 to nearly 1000 BC from their surroundings, but the dates are little more than guesstimates which may, with luck, place them within a century or two, but may, like a sherd from Lachish, leave them suspended anywhere between 1800 and 1200 BC. Nevertheless, it seems that the older Proto-Canaanite finds tend to be further south. Information about, and use of, the alphabet seems to have been drifting north, spreading out through Canaan ahead of the Israelites, or perhaps with them as they filtered into these richer lands. It was this system that found its next refined expression, not in letters, but in a different system entirely.

On a spring day in 1928, a Syrian farmworker named Mahmoud Mell az-Zir was ploughing his smallholding half a mile inland from the eastern Mediterranean coast. The farm lay an hour's walk north of Latakia (ancient Laodicaea), within sight of a small bay named Minet el-Beida ('White Harbour' after the white rocks that guard its entrance) where a few fishing boats worked. The piece of land caught the rain before the mountains to the east, the Jabal an Nasayriyah, sucked the clouds dry. It lay near an olive orchard which flanked a 60-ft hillock, of no use to anyone except as an occasional source of wild fennel that grew among its covering of scrubby bushes and lank grasses. As Mahmoud urged his horse forward, his ploughshare struck a large piece of rock. Trying to remove it, he scratched away the soil, and revealed a flagstone. He raised it and found himself staring into darkness. He had opened the way into an ancient tomb, and to a lost world which would prove to have peculiar significance for the history of the Bible, of Homer, and of the invention that underpinned the survival of both: the alphabet.

Syria had been under French administration since the end of the First World War, and Mahmoud knew that the French were keen on antiquities. Besides, people had sometimes found ancient artefacts, some of gold, in the nearby olive orchard, which fetched a good price. Nervously, he climbed in. Staring round in the half-light, he saw the place was as good as empty. It had been opened by tomb-robbers long ago, who had left nothing but a few small artefacts. He gathered them up and sold them to a local dealer. He told his master about the tomb. The local police heard. A report was made, which eventually landed on the desk of the French governor. He passed it on to the Antiquities Service whose director, Charles Virolleaud, sent a member of his staff, Leon Albanèse, to check out the find. Albanèse made a plan of the empty tomb and area, and delivered a low-key report to his boss, who forwarded it to the Louvre in Paris.

That might have been the end of the matter, if René Dussaud, Keeper of the Department of Oriental Antiquities, hadn't spotted similarities between the tomb, which seemed to date from about 1250 BC, and similar finds in Crete. He also knew the place himself, knew that a local legend spoke of a great city and that when the Turks ruled Syria they had sent archaeologists to comb the area, but found nothing. Dussaud had suggested in a book that the little bay might actually be the place mentioned as a port the Greeks knew as Leukos Limen, which like the Arabic name, also means 'White Harbour'. Here, perhaps, was proof that he was right, for a necropolis of that size was unlikely to exist on its own. It suggested that at some time there should have been a rich community in the area. And that little mound, Ras Shamra, 'Fennel Hill' as the locals called it, could hide something. Dussaud set up an expedition under the thirty-year-old Claude Schaeffer, then working in the Strasbourg museum.

A year later, in March 1929, Schaeffer and his team of five arrived in Latakia. Cars couldn't make the trip overland, so he hired seven camels, arranged for a detachment of twenty soldiers as a protection against bandits, and started work in early April, using soldiers and then locals as a workforce. As Dussaud had suspected, the tomb was not alone. It was part of a necropolis, a whole cemetery. Soon, Schaeffer's team unearthed an 8½ inch (20 cm) statue of Baal, the Middle Eastern storm-god, standing as if wielding his thunder-club and lightning-spear, and a little Greek-style ivory lid showing a fertility goddess, bare-breasted and full-skirted, holding ears of corn. Schaeffer sent an excited radio message to Paris: 'The treasure of Minet el-Beida is found!' In fact, this hardly amounted to treasure. But it was enough to summon the eminent Dussaud to the site. A necropolis suggested there should have been a city nearby. Perhaps, he suggested, Ras Shamra concealed it.

Almost at once, as Schaeffer's workforce cut into the hillside, they hit stones blackened by fire, then a bronze dagger buckled by intense heat, and part of an Egyptian statue, the hieroglyphs of which showed it was carved some time in the late second millennium BC. Another cut revealed storerooms, and ceramics dating from around 1200 BC.

On 14 May, after a week of digging, the team found some little clay tablets in a corner of a storeroom. They were covered with Akkadian cuneiform, but some of the tablets were in a type of cuneiform that no one recognized. A few days later, as the team opened another part of the hill, they hit a cache of bronze weapons and tools, many of which had the same writing on them. Work continued, revealing the remains of temples, houses, and a library with tablets by the thousand.

No one had a clue what this place was or who had built it. The key to the mystery surely lay in the little clay tablets in the unknown script. The work this mystery inspired was remarkable for several reasons: for its speed; for the generosity of the decipherers, who usually find their reward in being first; and for its significance. Those involved were about to discover an entirely unknown culture, language and script.

Back in Paris, Virolleaud got to work on the cuneiform

texts. Some were in Akkadian, some in the unknown
script. He noted that the script seemed to have only
about thirty different signs, too few to record syllables. It
had to be an alphabet. Moreover, one frequent sign
seemed to mark word breaks. If so, the words were all
short, which suggested that the script did not use vowels,
only consonants. Some tablets, which looked like letters,
began with a single sign. In other cuneiform scripts,
letters often began 'To so-and-so'. Perhaps this was an
equivalent of 'to'. He published the evidence, carefully
transcribed, in late 1929 – generosity that contrasts with
the actions of Arthur Evans, the discoverer of Minoan
Crete, who had kept many of his finds to himself in the
hopes of being the first to decipher them.

At this point the trail split. Two Semiticists seized on
Virolleaud's paper. One was a Frenchman working in
Jerusalem, Edouard Dhorme; the other a German in
Halle, Hans Bauer. Both were well qualified to crack
codes, because both had been cryptographers in the First
World War. Then they had been working against each
other, though unaware of each other's existence; now,
instead of vying with each other in secrecy, they helped
each other forward.

First off the mark was Bauer, a fifty-one-year-old professor of oriental languages. Besides being a wartime code
cracker, he had honed his skills working on the Sinaitic
inscriptions. From the length of the words in Virolleaud's
copies, he guessed the language was Semitic, because

scripts that record languages related to modern Arabic
and Hebrew omit vowels and thus have shorter words
than European languages. In Hebrew and its relatives 'to'
is '*la*'. So that initial sign could be an '*l*'. Then he saw lists
that could be names, many of which came in groups of
three words. The middle one was always the same. If this
script followed the usual Semitic pattern, common in
biblical names, this could be *ben*, ('son of'). Now he had
b, *n* and *l*. And since the *n* and *t* were equally common in
suffixes and prefixes, by eliminating the *n*s he identified
the *t*. Armed with these assumptions, he spotted b-^{c}-l-t –
Baalat, the feminine version of the god Baal, exactly the
same combination that Gardiner had identified in Proto-
Sinaitic in 1916. Patterns in what Bauer assumed were
numerals gave him other letters. In all, Bauer identified
twelve consonants and three versions of *a*, which was not
our *a*, but a glottal stop. It had taken him just a week, and
he dashed off his conclusions in a letter to Dussaud in
Paris, and an article to his local paper.

Meanwhile, Dhorme was covering similar ground. In a
flurry of publications that summer, both corrected each
other's errors, both acknowledging each other's work.
And Virolleaud, on the receiving end of yet more tablets,
searched for and found three signs that could mean
'king', *m-l-k* in many Semitic languages. By October, the
task was virtually complete. A new script was in the
public domain, and a long-forgotten Phoenician–
Canaanite culture on the point of resurrection.

What culture, though? In 1931, Schaeffer himself, now into the second year of digging, spotted the word *g-r-t*. The addition of three vowels suggested to him that he was exploring the remains of the capital of a mysterious state known from Egyptian sources as Ugarit. So it was. The several thousand cuneiform tablets – treaties, letters, literary works, inventories – now unearthed have shown that the Ras Shamra mound lay at the centre of a Phoenician city-state whose roots stretched back 6000 years, rising to a golden age of temples, palaces and shrines between about 1500 and 1200 BC. As yet, there is no formal history, because meanings are obscure, dating controversial and context often impossible to establish. But in the intervening years a quarter of the city has been opened, and tourists now wander the streets and waist-high walls. Since Ugarit chose to write its records in clay rather than papyrus, enough details are known to bring Ugarit to life.

Ugarit covered some 1300 square miles, an area the size of Kent, a little larger than the state of Rhode Island, reaching some 20–30 miles inland at its height in the late second millennium BC. Scattered across it were some 200 villages, with 100 or so inhabitants each. Its palace had 90 rooms, including a verandah'd garden, a scriptorium and bakery for producing clay tablets. Measuring some 10,000 square metres – 100 metres across – the palace was one of the grandest structures of the Middle East. Through its port, today's mostly deserted

White Harbour, it became a hub of international trade, linking Greeks, Egyptians and Cypriots. Its artisans became famous as workers of bronze, imported from Cyprus.

Overland, Ugarit dealt with a succession of empires and kingdoms to the north and east. Seven different scripts in four languages show how cosmopolitan the place was. Diplomatically, it steered a precarious course as a buffer state between the two rival empires, the Hittite empire (Khatte) to the north and Egypt to the south, balancing grand strategy with the demands made by smaller, local kingdoms and tribes. In this ancient equivalent of the great game of Anglo-Russian imperial diplomacy in nineteenth-century Asia, Ugarit played the role of a Persia or an Afghanistan, surviving by diplomacy and trade, swopping princesses and high-born women in marriage, exchanging ambassadors, making and remaking treaties, now ally, now colony, now independent kingdom.

Diplomacy failed in about 1340 BC, when an anti-Hittite alliance among Ugarit's neighbours inspired the Hittite ruler to offer fraternal 'assistance' to Ugarit's ruler, Niqmaddu II. From charred remains in the ruined palace, it seems likely that the alliance staged a pre-emptive strike, burned the palace and forced a Hittite retaliation. In any event, Ugarit fell into the Hittite fold. Egypt and Khatte re-established the old balance with a peace treaty in 1258 BC, and Ugarit, still under Hittite overlordship but now the centrepoint of trade between the two empires, prospered as never before. Some fourteen ships, used for both commercial and military purposes, their range limited by the watchful Hittites, carried out grain, vases and statues, and returned with minerals, oil, wine and slaves.

Wealth brought its own problems. Ugarit's outlying districts, where borders were vague and much disputed between governments, were happy hunting grounds for bandits and kidnappers, as revealed by international treaties and local judgements that decreed compensation for murdered merchants. In one case, a merchant named Talimmu sued the northern frontier town of Apsuna for the murder of his partner at the hands of the local mafiosi, and won: the town paid him a talent of silver.

Ugarit lay smack on the crossroads of east Mediterranean trade, and its thousands of tablets have revealed a rich intellectual life, all recorded in its own script. The scribes of this city were fluent in writing Akkadian, a vital script for international relations, yet they chose their own, apparently after toying with two separate traditions. Evidence for the first comes from a small clay tablet found at Beth Shemesh in 1933, which seems to be a cuneiform version of the Arabic alphabet beginning *h-l-ḥ-m*. Beth Shemesh is two hundred and fifty miles south, way beyond the borders of Ugarit; but in 1988 a Syrian–French expedition found a similar tablet in south-east Ugarit, providing a link between Ugarit and the twenty-two letters of the South Arabian alphabet. It looks as if the Ugaritians picked up on the alphabet as it started its migration north, without fully working out how best to adapt it.

Later, once the idea of the alphabet had taken hold in the Ugaritic heartland, someone realized it should be adapted better to the language, added another eight letters, and revised the order of the letters in accordance with Canaanite precedents. That order was revealed in 1949, with the discovery of a tablet in which the letters of the full thirty-strong Ugaritic alphabet were written in sequence. It was the equivalent of a school exercise book. In the schools of Ugarit, children learned their cuneiform version of the alphabet – and they did so in a sequence of peculiar significance, for most of the letters are ours as well as theirs. Leaving aside the letters that represent Ugaritian sounds, the sequence, transcribed into Roman script, was, in part:

a b d h j k l m n o p q r s t v

A culture that vanished utterly from history, with a script few can read even today, turns out to contain a strangely familiar trait.

And many other strangely familiar traits as well, because Ugaritic literature invigorated the very people from whom they had taken the idea, if not the form, of the alphabet. We know this because of the texts that survived thanks to the work of its priestly scribes, in particular one whose status was such that he signed his name, Ilmilku the Sacrificer, at the end of a cycle of Baal myths now known as the Story of Keret. The work of Ilmilku and his colleagues reveals that Ugarit's alphabetically based literature became part of a common literary tradition, and eventually, three or four hundred years later, infused that of the Hebrews. Perhaps that should be no surprise as Ugaritic and Hebrew were closely related languages, yet it still seems to some an affront to see the roots of the Old Testament in a rival culture, especially one as assertively pagan as this.

One poem, a sacred marriage hymn, describes how the Canaanite god of gods, El – the god of Abraham before he was transformed into Yahweh – marries two women. Its graphic images (as translated by Nicolas Wyatt) recall the Song of Solomon, while its mention of desert wanderings ending in something very like a promised land seems to mirror the Israelites' own sojourn in the wilderness:

El's penis grew as long as the sea,
Yea, El's penis as the ocean.
El took the two inflamed ones . . .
And lo, the two wives cried out
'O husband! Husband! Lowered is your staff,
Drooping the rod in your hand!'
He stooped: their lips he kissed.
Oh, how sweet were their lips,

> As sweet as pomegranate;
> From kissing came conception,
> From embracing, impregnation.

El urges the sons that are born of this union:

> Raise up a dais in the holy desert,
> There you will make your dwelling among
> The stones and trees.
> For seven whole years . . .
> The gracious gods went to and fro on the
>   steppes;
> They roamed the edge of the desert,
> And they met the guardian of the sown land,
> And they cried out to the guardian of the sown
>   land:
> 'O guardian! Guardian! Open up!'
> And he made an opening for them,
> And they entered.

Scholars point to many other instances of Ugaritic influence on the Bible. Psalm 29, for instance, is a glorious paean to God as a force of nature: 'The voice of the Lord is upon the waters: the God of glory thundereth', and also breaks the cedars, makes them to skip like a calf, shakes the wilderness and makes the hinds to calve. Transposed into Ugaritic, this is a portrait of the thunder-god, Baal. It looks as if the Hebrew poet has been inspired by, perhaps even plagiarized, a Ugaritic source. Psalm 104 offers similar links. God's attributes – the creator, who makes the clouds his chariot, whose ministers are flame and fire, whose voice is thunder – were also those of Baal. Possibly the Hebrew poet's aim was twofold: to assert the difference between the Hebrew God and the pagan Baal, yet at the same time to establish resonances and offer reassurance that the new vision could encompass the old.

Perhaps the most intriguing link concerns the oddest of Jewish dietary rules, that a kid shall not be 'seethed' (boiled) in its mother's milk. This apparently eccentric injunction, mentioned twice (Exodus 23:19 and Deuteronomy 14:21), has always challenged commentators. Who on earth would dream of doing such a thing? How much milk do you need to seethe a kid anyway? Some have struggled to find a hygienic purpose, or guess that it is an example of extreme cruelty. The great twelfth-century scholar, Maimonides, in his *Guide for the Perplexed*, suggested it was probably a ban on some idolatrous practice. A Ugaritic tablet supports him, with an order to cook a kid in milk as part of some ritual. It seems that the Pentateuch bans the practice simply because pagans did it when worshipping Baal – an assertion of Hebrew religious identity expressed as a dietary ruling.

Ugarit's golden age came to a sharp end in about 1200 BC for several reasons. The relationship with Khatte soured, perhaps because of a famine in both Khatte and Ugarit. Both needed grain shipments from Egypt, and one port of entry would have been Ugarit. In any event, Ugarit's king, Ammurapi, tried to restore the old rapport with Egypt, and the pharaoh responded with a rich consignment of luxury goods. Khatte was outraged at this perceived attempt to subvert a satrap. A letter orders Ugarit to send grain: 'It is a matter of death or life.'

But the nail in Ugarit's coffin came from the so-called Sea Peoples, whom the Ugarit archives refer to as Sikila, 'who live on ships'. Their origins are obscure, but they seem to have poured out of mainland Greece, from about 1300 BC onwards. By about 1220 BC, the great culture of Mycenaean Greece had fallen. The Sea People spread south and eastwards, bringing anarchy and destruction, aiming towards the treasure-house of Egypt. 'Now the ships of the enemy have come,' reports one letter from the Ugaritic archives. 'They have been setting fire to my cities and have done harm to the land.' In fact, the threat was to all the mainland powers, Egypt included. At some point, an invasion by sea and land threatens both Ugarit and Khatte. Khatte again demands aid. Another letter asks for 150 ships – a vast fleet that Ugarit could never have supplied. Ugarit refuses. An army marches south, and a general begs for help: how can he confront the enemy with only his wife and his children? But the city looks only to itself, for there a final crisis looms. A foreman tells his master: 'There is famine in your house, we shall starve to death. If you do not hasten to come, we shall starve to death. A living soul of your country you will not see.' One man writes to his lord: 'When your messenger arrived, the army was humiliated and the city was sacked. Our food on the threshing floors was burnt and the vineyards were also destroyed. Our city is sacked! May you know it! May you know it!'

And then all is silence, except for what the soil holds: evidence of a huge fire that left remains up to six feet thick, arrowheads, caches of weapons and tools, and no skeletons. Apparently, the people had time to flee, but no time to load up all their valuables as the city burned. Ugarit never recovered. Trade moved elsewhere. Dust slowly filled the streets and drifted over the tumbling walls, to be fixed at last by scrub and fennel into the concealing mound of Ras Shamra.

Ugarit's collapse was not mirrored to the south. These other Phoenician cities, most importantly Byblos, Sidon, and Tyre, must each have made their own accommodation with the threat. They were no doubt aided by an Egyptian victory over the Sea Peoples in about 1175 BC, but still had to reckon with a new power in the region, a coastal settlement of the tribe soon to be known as the Philistines. With Sea Peoples pressing in from north and south, with Israelites spreading through the Canaanite tribes inland, the Phoenicians saw their domains reduced to a rump. They had little alternative but to turn seaward, with greater vigour than previously, pursuing markets across the Mediterranean and beyond, to West Africa, Brittany, perhaps Britain. By 1000 BC, they were everywhere; yet they remain strangely obscure. Perhaps because they lacked a national identity, feeling themselves apart from their Canaanite fellows inland, these assertive individuals were unassertive about their culture (as mayors often are – witness the egotistical independence of American mayors like La Guardia, Daley, and Giuliani, petty kings in all but name). They were great artisans: the objects they made and traded have been found all over the ancient world, but they had no records (where would they have been kept?), no historians, no poets, no writers, at least none known so far. One of the major problems in researching the Phoenicians is that they wrote on papyrus, which doesn't keep well. Another is that their cities, on their excellent sites, have remained cities to this day, and the ancient remains are buried under brick and concrete. Much of the evidence is circumstantial, emerging from trade goods found scattered round the Mediterranean and references in the writings of other cultures. Scholars must become detectives. One small item, a dog-eared papyrus in Moscow's Museum of Fine Arts, throws a spotlight on a time, a place, two people, and Phoenician writing habits. In what follows, I have intensified the drama a little, but I stick to the original narrative, and the quotations are translated from the hieroglyphic original.

Around 1100 BC, when Egypt was still a 'broken reed', as the prophet Isaiah put it, from the assault of the Sea Peoples, an Egyptian purchasing agent named Wen-Amon, from the temple of Amon in Karnak, came to Byblos to buy timber for the 'great and august barque of Amon-Re, King of the Gods'. As Wen-Amon recorded in his own words, he had a tough journey. There was no official ship to bring him. Carrying along a statue of Amon as a talisman, he bought passage in a Syrian vessel. Most of his money was stolen en route in a Philistine port. He seized some Philistine silver in an act he justified as compensation, and fled on to Byblos, arriving as little more than a fugitive, without a ship of his own and without money.

The king, Zakar-Baal, was extremely acerbic, as one might be if beset by Philistines and Israelites, if one is responsible for a little city looking to one for survival, and if some tinpot official from a decaying power dumps himself on one's doorstep. 'I spent 29 days in his harbour,' recalled Wen-Amon bitterly, 'while he spent the time sending to me every day to say: "Get out of my harbour!" ' Finally, the king relented, and gave the agent a chilly reception, in an upper room, silhouetted in regal splendour against a panoramic view of the ocean. Where were Wen-Amon's documents? the king demanded.

What did he want? Timber, eh? And what made him think he had any chance of success?

But, stuttered Wen-Amon, your fathers used to . . .

'Of course they did! And if you pay me something I will do it! But my fathers performed this service only after Pharaoh – l.p.h. [shorthand for the ritual prayer for *life*, *prosperity* and *health*] had despatched six cargo boats laden with Egyptian products . . . And you? What have you brought with you?' – knowing of course that Wen-Amon was on his uppers – 'I am not your servant, nor the servant of him that sent you! What are these silly trips which they have made you make?' By this time, Wen-Amon would have been made aware that Zakar-Baal has an Egyptian servant with a very similar name, Penamon. Imagine Zakar-Baal's implied message: when you get home, if you ever do, you can tell your master that I use Egyptians as *butlers*.

Wen-Amon did his best. It wasn't true! This was not a silly trip! The king should remember that Amon is great, and the sea is Amon's, and Amon was the lord of Zakar-Baal's fathers, 'and you – you are also the servant of Amon', and he, Wen-Amon, was on Amon's business, and Zakar-Baal had made Amon – Amon-of-the-Road, the statue he had brought with him – spend 29 days in the harbour, and if only Zakar-Baal would provide a messenger, Wen-Amon would be able to send for the goods he needed to do the deal.

Zakar-Baal relented. After all, business was business.

Wen-Amon got his messenger, sent his message, and finally received his supplies, in rather impressive quantities: gold, silver, 10 bolts of linen, 500 papyrus rolls, 500 cowhides, 500 ropes, 20 sacks of lentils, 5 baskets of fish. The deal was done. Zakar-Baal set 300 men to fell the timber, season it, and drag it to the beach.

And now, said Zakar-Baal in a concluding interview, you better get out, unless you want to share the fate of some other Egyptian messengers, who spent 17 years here, and ended up dead. Just to emphasize the point, he turned to his Egyptian butler, Penamon: 'Take him and show him their tomb!'

No, no, said Wen-Amon, no need. I'm off. But really, he added (imagine him backing towards the door of that upstairs room with its commanding view of the ocean, talking nineteen to the dozen), you should have a stele inscribed and put up, and the stele should commemorate the fact that Amon-Re sent his messenger, Wen-Amon, and the great Zakar-Baal cut timber for Amon's great and august barque, and then loaded it up, and caused it to reach Egypt, and that's a deed good enough to ask for another 50 years of life, and then some other messenger will come and see the stele and know just how great you are.

A silence, perhaps. Hm. Wen-Amon wasn't such a bad fellow, after all. The two parted in something like friendship. Wen-Amon went down to supervise the loading of his timber . . .

. . . and at that moment 11 Philistine ships appeared. Wen-Amon knew why they were there – to arrest him for seizing his 'compensation'. This was the last straw. 'I sat down and wept,' he wrote, and at last got some sympathy. The king's scribe found him and asked what was wrong. Wen-Amon, who had now been away from home over a year, stared up tearfully at a flock of birds migrating southwards. 'Look at them,' he said to the scribe. 'How they travel to the cool pools! But how long shall I be left here?' The scribe reported back to Zakar-Baal, and Zakar-Baal took pity. He sent his scribe back with two jugs of wine and a ram, and a message: 'Eat and drink! Don't let your heart take on cares!'

Pity was one thing, politics another. Zakar-Baal did not want to antagonize anyone. Best get both parties out of Byblos, as soon as possible, before there was real trouble. He told the Philistines he couldn't have Wen-Amon, a royal and priestly messenger, arrested. But he was not going to fight for his release either. His solution was machiavellian: he ordered his crew to get the ship, with Wen-Amon aboard, out of harbour, and told the Philistines: you want him? Go get him! What happened on the high seas was not his affair.

As intended, Wen-Amon's Byblian crew got him safely away, only to be swept by contrary winds into another scrape. They made landfall in Cyprus, where locals seized them. Wen-Amon escaped and ran into town to the palace where he threw himself on the mercy of the local ruler, a princess named Heteb. Through an interpreter, he used his old messenger-of-Amon ploy, and pointed out that Heteb would have both Egypt and Byblos to reckon with if she didn't look after both him and his Byblian crew. Heteb took the point. 'Spend the night,' she said, and . . .

. . . and at this tantalizing point the papyrus breaks off, leaving us to assume that somehow Wen-Amon made it back home, where he found the leisure to write up his account.

Embedded in this vivid tale is a clue to Phoenician writing habits, and to the absence of written evidence. The key material was papyrus, with which Byblos was virtually synonymous. It was so much the established distributor of Egyptian papyri that it gave its name to the Greek word for 'book' and to the first great book of the ancient world. Byblians naturally used it themselves. While scaring the daylights out of Wen-Amon, Zakar-Baal had sent for records of previous timber deals, to check the terms – royal records, kept in papyrus rolls. Papyrus is lightweight, easy to carry, and easy to write on, which made it ideal for wide-ranging businessmen, but it is ephemeral, except in bone-dry conditions. Phoenician evidence for Phoenician life, recorded perhaps on some of the 500 rolls ordered by Wen-Amon, went to feed worms and fires.

Yet we can be certain of the script on the papyri that Zakar-Baal waved under Wen-Amon's apprehensive gaze, and fairly certain that it would have been the same script gracing the stele suggested by Wen-Amon, if Zakar-Baal had ever taken up the suggestion. It was a script that emphasized Byblos's determination not to kowtow any more to the great powers of the time, and show the lesser ones that his was no mean city. The Phoenicians rejected the baked clay tablets and cuneiform script of Mesopotamia, and of Ugarit, just a hundred miles to the north. Papyrus was an Egyptian writing material par excellence, but Phoenicians wanted nothing to do with Egyptian writing. They might have continued with their own version of hieroglyphic; but it, too, must have been a struggle to use. Anyone who knew both Egyptian and Semitic would wince at the distortions. What they needed was their own script to keep the motors of manufacturing, banking, import and export running, and record contracts, civil law, court cases galore.

By 1300 BC, a simpler notion was in the air, the sign-for-a-sound system used by Ugarit to the north and by those 'Asiatics' migrating into Canaan from Egyptian lands. Any literate person trading with Ugarit before its destruction in 1200 BC would have known that their scribes had seized upon the idea of the alphabet and adapted it. The Ugaritic solution wouldn't work for more southerly cities, because they did not use clay tablets and cuneiform. The answer was to take over the Canaanite system, and refine it, incidentally keeping roughly the same sequence of letters. Soon afterwards the Byblian pseudo-hieroglyphs vanished into the limbo of undeciphered scripts, awaiting the discovery of a bilingual source.

The results were no doubt recorded on papyrus that quickly mouldered away. The earliest known texts in Phoenician writing consist of letters on arrowheads, bowls and sherds of uncertain date and a few words carved on the large stone sarcophagus of one of Zakar-Baal's successors, Ahiram, who may have lived in the eleventh century BC. The inscription, clearly copied from letter forms that must have been well-established by writing on papyrus, was carved by Ahiram's son, Ittobaal, 'when he placed him in the house of eternity'. Ittobaal adds a curse on any ruler daring to open the tomb: 'May the sceptre of his rule be torn away, may the throne of his kingdom be overturned, and may peace flee from Byblos!' It was a warning which seems to have impressed the stonemason, for there is a graffito in the shaft of the tomb warning off graverobbers: 'Beware! Behold there is disaster for you under this!'

However it happened, the Phoenician alphabet of twenty-two letters written from right to left worked. Many cultures which were not in thrall to empires that wrote in cuneiform or hieroglyphic saw the advantages. Phoenician became a language of prestige, as did its script. By 900 BC, half a dozen neighbouring peoples were using the same system to write their own languages.

Aramaic and Hebrew both took over the script whole-sale, despite having extra consonants which did not exist in Phoenician. It spread westwards with Phoenician colonists to north-west Africa where it became the script of Carthage, outliving that city's destruction in 146 BC. Examples of Phoenician inscriptions have been found from every corner of the Mediterranean and far down the Nile, stretching over a thousand years, often in free-flowing forms derived from handwritten styles, finally dying out only in the third century AD.

It was at an early point in the process of expansion that some smart Greek traders, undergoing their own revival after a time of decay, also saw the advantage of the Phoenician system, and the alphabet took its next leap forward.

7

THE SELFISH ALPHABET

At about this point in my research, I began to wonder what was going on. Something new was on the loose, and it was spreading. It looked to me rather like an infection, if you can imagine such a thing as a beneficial infection. It was as if humanity were a single organism, and had been injected with a slow-acting brain-drug that enhanced performance. To work effectively, though, it had to achieve a certain level of efficiency in a certain number of this creature's cells to achieve take-off, rather like the explosion that occurs with new electronic products, faxes, mobile phones and pcs: a huge investment, an expensive high-status toy, a slow spread, growing acceptance, a price drop and *whoomf!* – we're all infected.

You can tell this was a struggle for me. I tried three different analogies – bug, drug, product – in an attempt to understand this new invention and its dissemination. What I really needed was a Grand Unified Theory of Culture that explains creativity, human interaction, and progress, and generally tell me the meaning of it all. Pending that, I began to play with another idea that's on the loose.

If you're interested only in the history and find theorizing a pain, you could skip to the next chapter. But if you're still with me, let's look at the alphabet from the alphabet's point of view.

Ever since Darwin put evolution at the top of the agenda for biology over a century ago, historians have made comparisons between biological evolution and cultural evolution. (In fact, Darwin himself did, wondering whether the emergence and death of languages might be explained by a version of natural selection.) Both types of evolution are superficially similar in that both achieve ever higher levels of complexity.

Of course, there is no comparison in terms of hardware – parents do not physically transfer mental information to their children. Kids only acquire the cultural complexity developed by their parents as a result of teaching, conscious or unconscious, and they may or may not pass it on to their children. Biological evolution, with its unpredictable consequences, is driven in part by *random* recombinations and mutations, while in cultural evolution the recombinations and mutations are *intentional*, with equally unpredictable consequences – intentional, that is, if you believe in your own freedom from hidden forces in society and your own unconscious, but that's a whole other book. We all stand on the shoulders of our predecessors, and do not simply replicate their advances.

Another difference between biological and cultural evolution: biology operates forward in time, from parents to offspring in a tight causal chain that is time-dependent. Culture operates in all directions – forwards, of course, from parents to children, but also sideways between us all, and backwards, in that parents 'inherit' cultural information from their children (my daughter could teach her grandmother how to suck eggs, if she would only consider buying a laptop). This process is not necessarily time-dependent. A manuscript or piece of information or artefact has on many occasions revolutionized a culture simply by the fact of its arrival; today's news infects the world instantaneously.

Yet the comparison between biological and cultural evolution is seductive. There *is* a flow of mental information between people, and it *does* increase in complexity from generation to generation. If there is anything in the comparison, there should be some unit of information, the mental equivalent of a gene, as the biologist Richard

Dawkins suggested in a puckish aside in his 1976 best-seller *The Selfish Gene*. He called the unit a meme, a term he coined from the Greek root that gives us *mimic*, adapting it to sound something like 'gene'.

It was an idea whose time had come. The meme burst upon a world hungry for evolutionary analogies. Academics seized on it and thrust it into the limelight. When Dawkins came to check out his creation on the Internet some twenty years later, he found over 5000 references. Several books had explored the notion of 'memetics', which has its own web-journal. My Word 97 programme queries the validity of 'meme' with a wavy red underlining, but I doubt if Word 2000 will. In its next edition, the *Oxford English Dictionary* will confer formal existence upon the meme, defining it as 'an element of a culture that may be considered to be passed on by non-genetic means, esp. by imitation'.

Imitation is the key. Imitation is a peculiarly human activity, because only humans imitate new things. (Animals don't, on the whole, though this question is hugely controversial among animal behaviourists.) But there's more to it than that. Mere imitation may focus on practicality and technique, to the detriment of content. If a line of people each copies a drawing of St Paul's Cathedral from the previous drawing, the last one will not look much like St Paul's. But if, right at the start, there is a generalized instruction to copy the idea of 'church' or 'building' the idea is likely to survive the process of transfer. To take another example, in the teaching of tennis, only a certain amount can be achieved by teaching mere strokes. To inherit the tennis-meme properly, a pupil must climb a hierarchy of instructions: swing the racquet in such and such a way; hit the ball; hit the ball *over the net*; hit the ball over the net *very hard* – now we're getting into the inner game – with a *spin*, and in a place where your opponent isn't; and above all *win*, which can only be done by *not* copying your opponent's strategy. In the words of the psychologist, Susan Blackmore, in *The Meme Machine*, copying the product is not the most effective way of being 'memetic'. A high-quality meme is transferred by copying generalized instructions.

The theory of memes picks up on the idea that all systems evolve, given the presence of three factors: heredity, variation and selection. It proposes that ideas colonize minds, which become their environment. Minds copy memorable ideas, and act on them. The behaviour is such that the ideas survive, to be passed on (no blood relationship is implied, merely a flow of information through classroom, talk, any of the media). Sometimes an error occurs. If the idea is improved, it spreads further and faster, nurtured by expanding cultures and then, as those cultures reach their limits, either failing with them or leaping to some new host. Meme will rival meme, with those that are more successful at ensuring their own propagation outperforming others (as the alphabet out-performs Chinese writing outside China). Unlike gene–

189

gene rivalry, meme-based competition is not sexually based. Memes replicate in hyperspace – between the ears, in books, in conversation, on the Internet.

And all this without anyone really being able to say what a meme is! It sounds at first that it should be anything you can conceive of, a definition so wide as to be meaningless. But remember the conditions of variability and selectivity. A meme should contain information in the right amount to modify behaviour in some way. Words that children make up in games don't count. A library is too big. But a new word that proves useful, like 'meme', is OK; so is a book; or the first four notes of Beethoven's Fifth, made especially memorable as the BBC's introduction to its wartime broadcasts; or the whole symphony. Wheels and bows-and-arrows seem obvious candidates for meme-ship, but we also have to include big ideas like monotheism, or Christianity, which combine a bunch of memes into a 'meme-plex'.

If you find this still infuriatingly vague, remember that revolutionary ideas in science do not necessarily start with a knowledge of a mechanism, or even a coherent theory. Newton had no notion how gravity worked; all he did was describe its effects. Alfred Wegener did not know how continents drifted when he proposed his theory in 1912; it took another half century to come up with a mechanism that explained his observation. The idea of evolution long preceded Darwin's theory; and his theory predated by seventy years the hard science of genetics, which still contains many mysteries. Spelling out the whole human genome, a task which will be completed within a few years, will be only a start at understanding the massively complex ways in which genes interact. A DNA sequence that produces a protein that goes to make eyes blue is a long way from those blue eyes that you can't get out of your mind since you saw them across a crowded room at a party last Thursday night. If Darwinism has a way to go, the idea of the meme is in its pre-Darwinian infancy. Our inability to pin it down should be no surprise.

As an aside, the meme has some unnerving implications, if memes are as selfish as Dawkinsian genes. In this view, bodies are created by genes so that the genes can copy themselves and get passed on to offspring. (Not that the genes care one way or another: there is no intentionality in the way they operate. That's just the way they work, as a gas balloon 'wants' or 'tries' to rise.) People are the human genes' way of ensuring their own survival and reproduction. Where, then, is our individuality? In the same way, in the words of Daniel Dennett in *Consciousness Explained*, 'A human mind is itself an artefact created when memes restructure a human brain in order to make it a better habitat for memes.' The theory suggests that in the depth of our being, we are nothing more than a mass of competing beliefs and behaviours imposed upon us by selfish memes. Where, in this, does, free-will come in? Or is 'free-will' just another meme, seducing us so that we can pass it on?

Now all of this may be nothing but theory, with a spurious appeal based on the genetic analogy. Many critics have dismissed the whole idea as vapid, as a misleading metaphor which suggests a way of understanding cultural change that has no foundation in reality. Perhaps the meme will go the way of phlogiston, the 'element' of which fire was supposedly made in the eighteenth century, and evaporate with the changing times.

Yet some novelties do seem convincingly like mental genes. It seems to me that the alphabet is a prime candidate for meme-ship, as a brief history of the early alphabet shows.

A vital mutation occurs, as part of the set of memes that form Egyptian hieroglyphic. A new environment presents itself: a disaffected, independent culture ready for colonization. Technically, the task of recording could have been done in cuneiform, or hieroglyphic, or even Chinese. But an established script implies an established culture, which is precisely what an alphabet meme does not need. It seeks a small, fringe society, a shrew-like, mammal-like culture sneaking about among dinosaurian giants, unconsciously awaiting its moment. In one group of Asiatics, the meme finds a suitable host. It jumps cultures. It ensures that it prospers by welding rival clans together and working symbiotically with a second set of memes, which we now label monotheism, underpinning a belief system that intensifies a growing sense of identity and self-assurance. Soon, with its host, the alphabet has a new geographical base in which it can replicate safely. Along the way, it senses the presence of other possible hosts, and spreads, virus-like, separating from its symbiotic companion, battening on to a society that develops fast in literary skills – the Greeks, the subject of the next chapter. (Later, that 'monotheism meme', finding its future limited by the very society that it has helped create, will leap away via Christ, St Paul and Mohammed to colonize other hosts, in a steady expansion that will take another 2000 years to reach its limits.)

All of this can be put in more generalized terms that make the alphabet even more gene-like. It is an idea which escaped from its original environment, colonized a new one, got itself copied pretty accurately, mutated so that it worked better and then, in many sub-forms, exploded through human societies until limited by competition with other societies and other writing systems. Like its ancestor, language, and its parent, writing, it multiplied the means of communication, building complexity, intensifying the impact of human culture.

The alphabet has a strange affinity with the very idea of the meme, which suggests to me that memes are here to stay. Both meme-theory and the alphabet are 'hyper-memes' (I think I just invented that piece of jargon, but I bet I'm not the first). When imposed on the flow of information from person to person (i.e. on other memes) they reduce the process to something that looks comprehensible. And in our desperate efforts to make sense of life, the universe and everything, the impression of comprehensibility counts for a lot. I have a suspicion that meme-theory may turn out to be a useful tool in making sense of cultural advance, and that the alphabet will be good evidence for its usefulness, perhaps even a catalyst that will help turn meme-theory into hard science.

Once upon a time Greek stories existed only in the mind and mouths of bards, and might have died with their singers. But when the idea of the alphabet caught on, the *Odyssey* was written down, Rieu translated it, and Mr Marshall read it to me, and here I am talking about it. This is a small consequence of the large change that is the subject of the next chapter, when the alphabet gave the accelerating spiral of cultural evolution one of its sharpest twists.

8

THE GREAT LEAP FORWARD

I n Mycenaean times there had been an extensive trade across the 800 miles that divided the Greek mainland and the Canaanite coast, forming one of the many sea routes linking Egyptians, Cretans, Hittites and Assyrians. Much of this trade fell away between the thirteenth and tenth centuries BC, when Sea Peoples menaced the coasts from the Aegean to Egypt. But during the late 900s, old links, which had never been completely broken, were restored. Canaanites, now reborn as Phoenicians, once again sailed westwards, passing Greek merchant seamen heading east; and at both ends of these journeys some made bases and eventually homes.

It was this exchange that gave the Greeks their alphabet,

of that they had no doubt. One story, mixing alphabet with cuneiform, said that the letters were merely returning home, because it was Hermes, the fleet-footed messenger of the gods, who had first written the sounds of speech as wedge-shapes; you can see them still being carried south by the cranes, as they migrate every autumn in wedge-shaped formations. But that was just a fable. Everyone knew it was really Zeus who started it, by falling in love with Europa.

In this tale, Europa ('broad face') is strolling along the Phoenician shore near Tyre. She is carrying a golden basket engraved with a heifer swimming in the sea. This is her past, and her future, for the beast is her great-great-grandmother, Io, once a priestess, then a heifer driven by a gadfly to cross sea after sea – leaving one part of the Mediterranean and its inhabitants, the Ionians, named after her – until at last she came to Egypt, where Zeus turned her back into a young girl and mated with her. Io's children later moved to Canaan, which is why Europa is walking the Tyrian shore, carrying the basket which reminds us (and should have warned her) that her destiny is tied to a bull, like the one that now gently accosts her. How is she to know it is Zeus, in love with his own descendant? He presents small gemlike horns. She decks him with flowers. He offers his back. She climbs on. He wanders to the shoreline, and suddenly he's in the turf, carrying her away to father more children and provide a name for Asia's rival continent. Her father,

Agenor, is outraged and sends off Europa's brothers to look for her. One is Phoenix (usually translated as 'Purple' though it can also mean 'palm tree') who sails to north Africa to found Carthage and give his name to the Punics, returning to the land named after him, Phoenicia. The second brother, Kadmos, heads for Greece. A cow leads him to Boeotia, pausing at a site where Kadmos sets up a shrine to the goddess Athene, and founds Thebes (not to be confused with the other Thebes on the Nile). There's lots more, of course – a serpent to be slain, dragon's teeth to be sown, a civil war to be witnessed – but those are other stories. Later Kadmos will marry Harmonia, daughter of the goddess Aphrodite, at a glorious ceremony that all the gods will attend. The couple will end up as snakes, like the harmless ones in the forests that used to cover Greece.

Herodotus, working in Athens in the fifth century BC, had all this in mind when he wrote of the origins of the alphabet, attempting to draw history from myth. He said it was brought by Phoenicians living on the island of Euboea, the largest island in the eastern Mediterranean after Crete. Euboea, divided from the mainland by a narrow channel, had originally been populated in part by Ionians, renowned seafarers who by the tenth century had begun to spread to the mainland and also had close links with the main Phoenician city of Tyre. As trade developed, Phoenicians established a Euboean headquarters in a little town on the site of present-day Lefkandi. It was from here, according to Herodotus, that Kadmos led an expedition westwards, settling across the strait in Boeotia and founding Thebes. 'These Phoenicians who came with Kadmos,' wrote Herodotus, 'brought with them . . . among many other kinds of learning, their script, which had been unknown before this, I think, to the Greeks.'

The story is widely accepted as containing some sort of truth, because Euboean artefacts have been found near Tyre and Phoenician artefacts at Lefkandi. Later, Greek letters came to be called both Kadmean and Chalcidic, after Euboea's capital, Chalcis. When all this happened, though, is a matter of recent controversy. Dates for the introduction of the alphabet into Greece ranged from 1050 to 750 BC. Only quite recently has it become possible to make some sense of the timing and mechanism of transmission.

It's fair to assume that Kadmos never existed. But myth often hints at realities hidden by time and distorted folk-memory. In this case, one reality is that during the second millennium BC the Mycenaean Greeks seized Crete, which under its previous Minoan rulers had worshipped the bull. Then, as Cretan Greeks, they attacked Tyre and abducted its women. If myth and history coincide at all, perhaps 'seduce' is a better word, for Europa was not entirely unwilling to be carried off by a god, and both language and archaeology suggest that the Greek–Phoenician relationship was of mutual benefit. A clue lies in the fact that Thebans were often described as 'Kadmeans'. *Kadm-* is not a Greek root; but it is a Semitic one. In Ugaritic, *qdm* can mean 'east', and the personal name *Qdmn* 'Easterner'. In the Bible, the *ben qedem* – 'sons of the east' – were the nomadic tribes of today's Jordan and Iraq. It sounds from the Greek names as if Phoenicians – Kadmaeans – could have set up a colony in Boeotia, and that this was enough to inspire the creation of an entirely mythical ancestor. Harmonia's name, containing the sense of anything joined, from bricks to musical notes, may originate with the Hebrew for 'citadel': *armon*. Might Kadmos marrying Harmonia be a mythic metaphor for Phoenicians 'marrying' the citadel of Thebes when they arrived with their new script?

Something is missing in all this. The link between Greece and Phoenicia is a little too neat. That 800-mile, two-week sea journey did not have to be done all at once. There were other islands along the way, including a major one, Cyprus, a mere 80 miles from Byblos, not much further from Tyre. It is to Cyprus that some scholars now look when they seek the point and the moment at which Greeks adopted the Phoenician alphabet.

So there could one day be another story, telling of a certain king who lived in a great palace in Cyprus around 800 BC. The king was a Greek, whose forefathers had arrived in Cyprus from the mainland two or three centuries earlier when outsiders forced them out. Greece, along with its sister culture in Crete, had fallen into barbarism and ignorance. But in Cyprus the memories of the great old days lived on. The king (the *wanax*, as he called himself, retaining an ancient title) loved songs, and feasting, and stories of the Greeks we now know as Mycenaeans, stories that were already many centuries old, of Achilles and the wily Odysseus, of the siege of Troy, of the days when gods dwelt among men.

These were no suffering exiles. Their nostalgia was a romantic gloss on a comfortable life, underpinned by trade across all the eastern Mediterranean. Cyprus, being so close to what is now Syria and Lebanon, was well placed to link present-day Syria, Turkey and Greece. In this the *wanax* and his Greek-speaking subjects relied heavily on outsiders, Phoenician newcomers who looked to their home on the mainland, and to the trading empire that linked Egypt, Italy, the Aegean islands, even the north African coast. Working out of their two main bases on the east coast, Enkomi and Kition, the Phoenicians had proved highly successful, in part because they kept good records with their peculiar script.

True, the Cypriot Greeks kept records, written in the local script which they had adopted soon after their arrival. They had found it preferable to their own system, known as Linear B, a complex of eighty-five signs and dozens of ideograms which had been in use for several centuries before the collapse of Mycenaean culture. The Cypriot system of fifty-five syllabic signs, adapted from an earlier script that so far defies decipherment, was easier to master than Linear B, but it was still somewhat challenging to a culture with no tradition of scholarship. Few Phoenicians bothered to learn it. Why should they? Their traders could scribble inventories on pieces of pottery, or papyrus scrolls, or waxed wooden tablets, or leather, all of which could be carried about or stored by accountants and treasurers. The Greeks lacked nothing in intelligence, trading acumen, or products – Cyprus was, after all, named for its copper deposits which had been a vital part of the region's economy for over 1000 years – but up against the Phoenicians they were at a disadvantage.

There was another reason to look to the Phoenicians for a new script. In both cultures, the wealthy liked to compose dedications on boundary markers, buildings and tombs. To have one's name in stone together with a suitably flattering piece of poetry was, after all, the closest one could come to immortalizing one's achievements. The Phoenicians worked easily with their consonantal script, which left the vowels to be determined by the reader. Surely it should be possible to borrow the Phoenician letters and adapt them to Greek in such a way that everyone, even Phoenicians, could know who was responsible for such-and-such a building, tomb or statue?

The king, an astute and ambitious fellow, commissioned

his most erudite scholar to adapt the Phoenician script so that it would record Greek. There is a consensus that, as the Kadmos myth suggests, adaptation would have been the work of one man, a sort of ancient-world Sejong. In the words of one expert, Barry Powell, the combination of changes 'places beyond doubt the conclusion that the alphabet was created by a single man at a single time'. Perhaps there was a commission of scholars. You can imagine the fuss, the long and heated deliberations, with bilingual advisers pointing out that both Phoenician and Greek had some sounds that did not exist in the other language. Obviously, merely taking over Phoenician letters would never work, because some of the Phoenician letters would be useless and some Greek sounds would be left with no letters. Why throw out a perfectly good writing system for this foreign invention?

No problem, came the counter argument, just use the same signs where possible, and give those left over to typically Greek sounds. Verse dedications demanded some such adaptation, because in Greek the vowels did far more than in the Phoenicians' Semitic language. To make Greek verse work, you had to know exactly what vowels to use and how long to sound them. Phoenician letters offered a number of possibilities. Take just one example: the first letter in the Phoenician alphabet, the glottal stop, *alep*. The Greeks didn't have this sound. But they did have vowel sounds that the Phoenicians didn't represent at all. Vowels are hard to pin down, and won't stay fixed for long but, as our more pedantic Greeks may have argued, no language can exist without them, even if they are not written. So here was a chance to improve on the Phoenician original. For instance, one of the Greek vowels was an '*a*'. Why not simply shove the two together, the Phoenician *alep*-sign and the Greek *a*-sound? So it happened that the Cypriot Greeks retained the first letter of the Phoenician system, with its Phoenician name, which was gibberish in Greek, but a name is a name, and one is as good as another. Anyway, even in Phoenician, *alep* had long since lost any obvious relation to its acrophonic origins. Imagine someone asking our adapter, 'Why is this called *alep*?', to which the impatient reply would be, 'I don't know. Why is a ship called a ship? That's its name, OK?' The second letter, the *b* with its *bayit* mnemonic, could stay unchanged, because the Greeks, like us, shared the *b*-sound with Phoenician. For fifteen letters, the origins were forgotten, the names kept, with the addition of a Greek *-a* ending (*alep* becomes *alpha*; *beyit*, *beta*).

Other 'spare' Phoenician consonants – *he, yod* and *ayin* – became the Greek *e, i* and *o*, while the Phoenician *wau* split in two to form both a consonant and a fifth vowel, *y*. There were other novelties as well, like a new *f*-sound, *phi*. The adapter didn't seem to be certain of the orientation of the letters, because several were rotated or inverted. And for a collection of four related Phoenician sounds and letters – roughly equivalent to *z*, *s*, *ts* and *sh* –

the adapter exchanged sound, name, letter shape and order. Here's what should have happened, if the adapter had made the most logical choices, compared to what actually happened:

Phoenician	Should have become	But actually became
Zai/z	San/s	Zeta/dz or sd or zd
Semek/s	Sigma/s	Xei/sh, later ks
Sade/ts	Zeta/dz	San/s
Sin/sh	Xei/sh	Sigma/s

Why these changes occurred has been the subject of highly complex research and arguments, incomprehensible to those unfamiliar with Arcado-Cypriot Labiovelar Palatalization and the like. But some details concern us here. Why, for instance, did *sh*, a sound that Phoenicians had but Greeks didn't, became *ks*? The *ks* combination could have been spelled perfectly well as k+s. Why a separate letter? One possible answer is that Cypriot had originally had a *ks* as part of its syllabary. A similar argument applies to the adoption of symbols for *ps* and *zd* (some classicists would rather Zeus is pronounced 'Zday-us', to the confusion of non-specialists like me). These snippets of evidence are as good a reason as any for placing the initial adapter, that 'genius and benefactor' as Barry Powell calls him, on Cyprus.

After making their adaptations, the commission presented their conclusions to their *wanax*. Phoenician letters, Phoenician names for the letters, and Greek sounds, with a few modifications. The first complete alphabet, vowels and all. In essence, the alphabet of the western world.

Perhaps. But the attempt to turn fable into history is fraught with academic controversy, fuelled in part by the one incontrovertible fact, that the Greeks began to write with Phoenician letters, with astonishing and momentous consequences. It would be nice to know when and how this happened.

First, the timing. Traditional dating depended on the timing of the switch-over from bronze to iron, which was widely accepted to have occurred about 1200 BC, and on various synchronicities between Middle Eastern cultures. But that left an odd gap about which virtually nothing was known. The Phoenicians had their alphabet by about 1100 BC, yet the first evidence of the Greek version appears only in about 800 BC. Why a 300-year delay? Traditionally, it was generally accepted that Greece entered a post-Mycenaean Dark Age of barbarism and illiteracy and that was that. More recently, the whole issue of this Dark Age has been up for review.

The problem can be focused on Cyprus. From the architecture and pottery, it seems that Cyprus fell into a black hole for two centuries before about 1000 BC.

Even large ports like Enkomi and Kition seemed to have ceased to exist, only reviving with the arrival of the Phoenicians in about 850 BC. Yet tombs of the period supposed to date from around 1000 BC indicate continuing prosperity; and the king of Tyre is said to have suppressed a revolt in Kition; and a Phoenician bowl found in Kition dates from about this time (apparently used in some religious ceremony, the bowl's fragments include the unnerving injunction: 'poke the dog so that it slumps before Astarte'); and the Cypriot syllabary re-emerged again after the supposed Dark Age; and Cypriot pottery is found in eleventh- to tenth-century Palestine. What are we to make of this Dark Age? It seems to be an age of paradox. A homeless population with wealth enough for rich burials; an empty town full of rebellious Phoenicians; an illiterate people who remember how to read; an impoverished population who make pots for export – none of it makes sense.

The problem came into even sharper focus with the discovery in 1979 of a statue in northern Syria, near the ruins of Tell (or Tall) Halaf, which in ancient times was an Aramaean city named in the Bible as Gozan. It includes a bilingual inscription in Assyrian cuneiform and the Aramaean alphabet. From the cuneiform it seems clear that it dates from about 850 BC. But the Aramaean letters look suspiciously like Proto-Canaanite which, if you recall, are supposedly dated three hundred years earlier, because they relate neatly to Egyptian chronology.

But that chronology itself lacks rigour. Historians accept that it could be dated to about a century either side of 1800 BC, and a few more radical scholars argue that it could be as much as three hundred years out. No one was particularly worried (and many specialists are not much worried even now) because Palestinian dating seemed to be on firm ground. Now it turns out there is nothing solid about the dating of any artefact in the whole region before about 800 BC. Trying to arrive at a balanced view is to juggle with half a dozen different cultures, all of which interact on each other. Perhaps in the end, that three hundred-year gap will evaporate, and the whole of eastern Mediterranean history up to 800 or so BC will compress, to reduce the Dark Age to something like two or three generations, short enough to be crossed by scripts and pottery techniques.

Running across this are the three great mysteries about the first alphabetical works, Homer's epic masterpieces, the *Iliad* and the *Odyssey*. The first mystery is Homer's identity, the second when he lived, the third when his epics were recorded. The works were so obviously great that, whenever they were recorded, post-Mycenaean society must surely have had a certain sophistication. That seems to run against the grain of a widespread popular assumption that literacy is the only sound basis for cultural complexity. How could there be a rich culture, if the poor benighted saps couldn't even read and write? How could a culture spring fully formed from a 'non-culture'? This question underlies a scholarly debate which has been running from 1795, when the German classicist, Friedrich Wolf, suggested that Homer was illiterate. Interest in various Homeric Questions intensified in the 1930s about when the Greeks adopted the alphabet, and when Homer either lived, or was written down, or both. The debate continues.

The archaeological evidence seems to suggest *c*. 800–750 BC as a date for the introduction of the alphabet, so that was when Homer's two epics may have been recorded; but the depth of Greek culture also suggests that the alphabet had to have arrived much earlier, in order to explain the richness of the Homeric world. Where were the primitive bits of alphabetical prose that must have preceded Homer? Works of genius just don't spring into being without foundations. Or perhaps the Greeks retained their more ancient writing system, the Linear B of their ancestors, the Mycenaeans? If this was so, where was the evidence? One suggestion was that everything was written on papyrus and vanished as Phoenician literature had. But how strange that absolutely no evidence had survived from this period, when it had from previous periods. In brief, had there been a Dark Age at all?

It is possible to resolve some of the paradoxes by revising

conventional attitudes about the nature of literacy. To define cultural depth in terms of literacy involves four assumptions:

- that alphabetic literacy must have spread from the top levels of society downwards;
- that the alphabet would immediately be considered a superior achievement, and be instantly taken up by anyone with a claim to intelligence and culture;
- that non-literate cultures are necessarily simple and inferior;
- that poetry is more refined than prose and must therefore come later.

Research into the nature of pre-literate cultures suggests that all these assumptions are false and should be replaced with their precise opposites.

It is, for a start, too glib by half to dismiss pre-literate Greek society as 'inferior'. Many of the foundations of the society that was to blossom in the fifth century were in place five hundred years earlier. The Greeks of 1000 BC forged iron and built wooden temples in styles that anticipated the later stone ones. In particular, they had moved away from tribalism and powerful overlords (like Agamemnon in the *Iliad*) to create the independent city-state, the *polis* that anchored Greek society for a millennium. These were tiny units, mostly no more than country town-sized in modern terms, dominating small plains set apart by mountain ranges. Possibly, the *polis* arose from the need to counter barbarians with fortified living sites and markets (*acropolis* means 'high town') rather as the Celts and medieval English did. This turned out to be a good size for self-sufficiency in a countryside where fields, orchards and rivers were equally spread out on all sides (unlike Egypt, strung out along the Nile, or Mesopotamia's two-river civilization). From this necessity the Greeks made a virtue: small was beautiful. Aristotle, writing in the fourth century, said that the population of a *polis* should be small enough to be addressed by a single herald. Five thousand citizens was an ideal maximum, which with women, children and slaves made a total of about 25,000. By Aristotle's day, practice had already outrun the ideal, giving Athens and its surrounding area a population of about 40,000 male citizens, or perhaps 200,000 in all. But if this was large in Greek eyes, no wonder the Persian empire seemed barbaric.

As a non-literate society of small groups united by culture and trade, pre-alphabetical Greece could only have been held together by person-to-person contact, formalized with some public statement made at an assembly. That is how behaviour was codified, transmitted and modified. Simpler, smaller groups may get along without formal meetings – the 600 members of the tribe with whom I lived, the Waorani of eastern Ecuador, lived in semi-nomadic groups of no more than a few dozen, and they had no need of chiefs or assemblies or public statements. But as societies increase in complexity, so does the need for formal ways of fixing memory and identity and rules of behaviour.

How was this to be done with due impact? Not by everyday speech, which is by its nature of the moment, and unmemorable. The message must be emotive, have a power which can only come from pithy statements, or verse, or powerful narrative, or words set to music, or all four in combination. These techniques distil meaning, and then emphasize that meaning with striking words, and with stylistic tricks that fix words into a pattern with rhythm, and sounds that echo each other. This is the most effective way to bind message, performer and audience.

It is poetry that we remember most easily. During my childhood in a Kentish village, guns were a part of my life, both for sport and necessity. When my father drummed the dangers into me, he probably said some-thing like, 'Now remember, don't point your gun at anyone, even if it isn't loaded.' If he did, I forget. What I remember is him quoting a little verse:

> Never, never let your gun
> Pointed be at anyone.
> Whether or not it loaded be
> Matters not the least to me.

These lines served me well when, at the age of eleven, I sneaked away from a party for younger children and into my Uncle Stephen's office. There, by chance, in a corner, I saw a rifle with telescopic sights my uncle used for shooting rabbits. I had never held a bolt-action .22 before, only an airgun. I picked it up, sat back in an armchair, fell in love with the weight of smooth wood and dark metal. I released a lever, pulled, felt the oiled bolt slide back, and pushed. Something clicked, leaving the bolt protruding. It was, I guessed, ready to fire, if it had been loaded. At this moment I realized I had no idea how to release the bolt without pulling the trigger. I couldn't leave it cocked. Uncle Stephen would know someone had been fooling with the gun. There was only one thing for it: to release the bolt by pulling the trigger. Uncle Stephen handled guns all the time. It couldn't possibly be loaded, because no adult would ever, *ever* leave loaded guns about. So by adult definition, there was no danger. Besides, I longed to see the bolt click forward. At that moment, the gun was pointing at the door. It was a thin wooden door. I see it now, a plywood panel with a dark frame, beyond which five-year-olds shrieked and laughed. '*Never, never let your gun*': the lines were as much a part of me as brown hair and blue eyes, so although I knew it to be unloaded, I pointed the gun into a corner, and pulled the trigger. The gun was loaded. That was the closest, I think, I came to death as a child, not from the bullet, which blew a hole in the plaster, bounced off the brick underneath, and vanished somewhere. It was the shock of it. I sat staring at the hole and the dust, my heart leaping like a wounded rabbit. An impossibility had happened, a universal law violated and I, a child, could have killed a child, if it had not been for four lines of doggerel.

Until the 1920s, Homer, as the author of the two most ancient texts of western literature, was seen by most as a *writer*, notwithstanding those who had claimed the opposite. Then a young American, Milman Parry, refining the point made long before by Wolf, became convinced that the *Iliad* and the *Odyssey* were not to be seen primarily as written works at all but as 'oral literature', a contradiction in terms that found little favour in Berkeley. After finding a publisher in France, Parry won backing from Harvard to test his idea by recording oral poetry as practised by illiterate bards in the coffee-houses of Serbia, Bosnia and Hercegovina. There he discovered that bards, passing songs from generation to generation, had an astonishing facility. It was not a question of memorizing vast chunks of text and delivering it, but of turning every performance into an improvisation, accompanying themselves on a one-string fiddle. In performance, a bard based each song on traditional themes and formulae – which accounted for 25–50 per cent of the 'text' – recombining, trimming and extending in response to the feel of the audience, always fitting the song into the same verse form (in this case, a line of ten syllables, with a caesura after the fourth), without pause and without relying so much on formulaic expressions that the audience became bored.

The research proved a tough task, because the bards followed no course of training and never analysed their own work. Like most illiterate people, they did not learn 'words' because they didn't know that their utterances broke down into words and lines. In short, they had no idea how they did what they did. The songs were simply part of their language. There was no received, or authentic version of an epic or its constituent stories. Astonishing feats of memory were displayed with casual ease.

One case concerned a master bard named Avdo Mededovic, whom Parry had been recording for weeks. Another bard named Mumin appeared, who sang a song several thousand lines long, which was new to Avdo. When asked his opinion, Avdo praised his rival, but said he thought he might sing it better, even though he had only heard it once. He then did so: 'The song lengthened, the ornamentation and richness accumulated, and the human touches of character . . . imparted a depth of feeling that had been missing in Mumin's version.' The quote is from *The Singer of Tales*, by Albert Lord, a student of Parry's, who took over his work when Parry was killed in a car crash in 1935.

Parry's work founded a new academic discipline, the study of orality, and a new way of looking at the impact of literacy. Thereafter, anthropologists recorded oral poetry wherever they could, and historians of literature began to analyse old texts – the Bible, *Gilgamesh*, Norse epics – for signs of orality.

But if Homer's epics were recited and sung, what was the purpose? Clearly, they were more than after-dinner entertainment. They were works of genius, designed to tell listeners where their roots lay and what made them what they were. To do this, they included vast amounts of information, so much that Eric Havelock called them 'tribal encyclopaedias'.

Take the start of the *Iliad*, which opens on a quarrel: 'Anger be now your song, immortal one.' The Greeks at Troy have sacked a nearby city and Agamemnon, the king, has seized a daughter of a priest of Apollo as a prize. He rejects an appeal by the priest to return her. Outraged, Apollo sends a plague, which a seer says can only be reversed if this girl is returned. Agamemnon is angry. She's his booty. He would have to be compensated. The great warrior Achilles points out there isn't any booty left. 'What things we took from cities when we sacked them have been distributed. It is not proper that the people should reverse this.' Agamemnon agrees, but in recompense seizes Achilles' own prize-girl. In a vicious row, the two almost fight. Achilles withdraws from the war. The arguments spreads to the gods, who dispute the legitimacy of the quarrel, the fight between the two leaders and the merits of Greeks and Trojans. The scene is set for the working out of Zeus's will.

This opening sequence interweaves several major social issues: the division of spoils, the nature of sacrilege, how authority is symbolized and upheld, how decisions are made by commanders, how princes should act. The social framework is set in a religious one. The gods have their traits, their functions, their places of worship, their rituals and sacrifices. But sacred and profane are not things apart. At Zeus's arrival in the divine dining hall, 'all the gods stood up together from their seats in the presence of their father'. Zeus is patriarch and prince as well as senior god. And as the tale progresses it includes numerous practical details of how ships are handled, cults practised, animals hunted, inheritance passed on, wives chosen, households managed, bodies buried, heroes lamented.

All of this body of law and practice can only be fixed in the mind by a narrative of great events and people and issues, intensified by style, metre, and memorable formulae, repetitions and verbal harmonies. It is these elements that create a sense of pleasure, that sense that children feel when language is new and words playthings. Performing a song, reciting a poem, repeating a mantra – all are aspects of what the Greeks called *mousike*, which was more than 'music': it was a craft that combined words, rhythm and song, in sub-specialities practised by the nine 'muses' who were known as the Daughters of Memory. In pre-literate Greece, the hidden purpose of poetry was to teach by entertaining; if it failed to entertain, it could not teach.

Evidence for all this, Havelock argues, comes from later opinions. Aristophanes in *Frogs* called the master poets of old 'the poets of utility'.

> As for the divine Homer
> Surely his honour and glory accrued simply
>   from this, that he gave needful instruction
> In matters of battle order, valorous deeds, arms
>   and men.

It was because Homer was seen as practical that some came to regard him and the reverence in which he was held with deep suspicion. Heraclitus was scathing: 'What Homer deserves is to be flung out of the window!' In Plato's *Ion*, a Homeric bard is ridiculed for claiming that he knows everything there is to know simply because he knows Homer. When Plato came to propose a reform of education, he reviled Homer as a mere 'composer of fictions'. If he had been anything more, surely he would have had disciples, as befitted a great teacher? No, he was no proper educational model. Of course he was a genius, but that was what made him dangerous. He should actually be banned, in favour of instruction better suited for the modern age.

Plato was judging Homer from the point of view of a literate society. But Homer's significance lies as much in pre-literacy as in literacy. His epics bridge the two worlds, and remain unique as *written* works that record *oral* roots. Tradition speaks of him as a bard, not a scribe. He makes one single reference to writing, in Book 6 of the *Iliad*, when a prince, Bellerophon, is sent off with a 'deadly cipher, magical marks' hidden in a 'folded tablet', instructions to the recipient, the Lycian king Iobates, to arrange for Bellerophon's death. The phrases suggest that Homer and his audience knew about writing, but not how to write, for the letter is a dramatic device with parallels in a Sumerian saga and the biblical story of David. How bard became author is unknown, for no one recorded the act of recording. Unlike Ilmilku, Homer never signed his works. Perhaps, as tradition claims, he was blind; if not, he would still not have done the work of transcription himself. How then is it possible to say anything of how these first great works in alphabetical script came to exist?

Only by looking at the indirect and circumstantial evidence supplied by archaeology and linguistic analysis.

Whether it came from Cyprus, or from Euboea, or direct from Phoenicia, the alphabet arrived on the mainland, and attached itself to a society at a crucial stage in its evolution – a youngish culture of enough separate units to create a healthy sense of rivalry without degenerating into anarchy, secure from foreign invasion, economically viable, complex enough and stable enough to build a sense of identity over several centuries, with no apparent loyalty to an established writing system. By 800 BC, then, it was a culture ripe for a literary revolution.

The earliest evidence of Greek literacy is a vase found near the Dipylon Gate in Athens in 1871. It was dug up illegally, when archaeology was little more than tomb-robbing, so it cannot be dated from the objects found with it. By its style, known as Late Geometric, it was made about 750 BC at the earliest. It's not much to look at, but it is famous because of what is written on it – Phoenician letters that form part of a sentence: 'Who of all dancers now dances most playfully, let him . . .' It is one line of verse (a hexameter) and part of another, which falls away into a scribble.

What does it mean?

Imagine the end of a dance contest, the winner recalling the herald's opening invitation and wanting some reminder for his family or his patron of what the pot means. He shouts to the crowd: 'Does anyone here know Phoenician writing?'

An eager hand reaches up, a builder, or trader, or visiting Phoenician. 'What should I write?'

'What the herald said: "Who now of all dancers dances most playfully, let him be rewarded with this pot." '

The man scratches with a sharp stone on the black paint. 'Look, now the pot speaks!' Then, as the hero grabs it from him – 'But I haven't finished!'

Too late; the winner is off, displaying his prize. Later, he sees, or someone tells him, that the sentence is

219

unfinished. He adds a letter or two, randomly, then gives up.

Or perhaps it wasn't like that. Perhaps the pot sits for years in the winner's house. In old age, he tells the story of his victory to his grandchildren. 'If this pot could speak, children, what stories it could tell.'

A teenage boy is listening. He is apprenticed to a potter who often adds little inscriptions to his work.

'But grandfather, pots *can* speak.'

'What do you mean, child?'

'Give it to me. I will make it speak. Tell me again what the herald said.'

And so, perhaps after fifty years, as 'Phoenician writing' spreads through Greece, a teenage hand scrawls the message, trailing off as memory or inspiration wane.

The imaginary boy was quite right about talking pots. They travelled far and wide. One also made around the same time was found on the island known today as Ischia, five miles out to sea from Naples. It was no paradise, for the giant Typhon occasionally shook the land as he tried to break out from his prison beneath its volcano, but its mineral-rich soil was good for vines and the north-west coast, with its two natural harbours, was a base for some 5–10,000 Greeks. Today it is part of the *comune* of Lacco Ameno. The Greeks called the place Pithekoussai, for reasons no one can explain. Perhaps it had something to do with monkeys (*pithekos*), or jars (*pithoi*), or some local name corrupted into Greek, as

World War I British soldiers turned Ypres into 'Wipers'. Its many graves, excavated from the 1950s onwards, included one of a ten-year-old boy who died around 725 BC. It contained the remnants of something rather inappropriate for a boy entering the underworld: a two-handled drinking cup, which from its shape was probably made in Rhodes. Around its rim runs a damaged inscription, which in literal translation runs, 'Of Nestor I am the well-drunk drinking-cup'. Perhaps this is a reference to wise old Nestor, king of sandy Pylos in Homeric tales, who owned a gold-studded cup so huge that ordinary men strained to lift it, 'but the old man could lift it with ease'. Or perhaps the proud owner was himself called Nestor. The inscription continues with a couplet in hexameters:

Whoever drinks from this cup straightway he
Will be seized with desire from fair-crowned
Aphrodite.

An image comes to mind. Nestor is well off, happy to spend money on good wine and pots that recall his legendary namesake. He is something of a party-goer, or to put it in Greek terms, a regular guest at symposia, which were not the austere intellectual gatherings suggested by the word today but drinking parties for upper-class men. Xenophanes, writing in the sixth century BC, described what they were like at their best. Washed, garlanded and perfumed, the participants would drink and sing of heroes and great deeds and the gods and love, the love in this case being the love of beautiful boys. As Margaret Williamson argues in *Sappho's Immortal Daughters*, Greek homosexuality was very different from today's. A man would brag in song about seducing a boy as proof of his own status as an active, dominant member of an aristocratic elite, and as a mentor of younger males. The boy, soon to be a fully-fledged citizen himself, would comply because the liaison would be useful socially or politically. Neither would necessarily be gay, in the modern sense.

This image of Nestor offering his cup to handsome teenagers sits oddly with the cup's final resting place. Nestor could have come from Rhodes, with his cup; or he could have bought it locally and had it engraved there; Pithekoussai no doubt had its symposia; but why would this object, with its lusty hints, be buried with a child? If this story could be told, it would, I think, be a sad one.

These two pots, from Athens and Pithekoussai, are evidence that the alphabet had arrived on the mainland and Greek colonies some time in the late eighth century. Both associate the alphabet with high status. But writing with Phoenician letters was not first and foremost the work of the high-born. There is nothing in eighth- to sixth-century BC Greece like the grand inscriptions of Egyptian pharaohs or Assyrian kings. Quite the opposite. It seems that writing, rather than being imposed from the top down, is a bottom-up activity, spread not by scholars but artisans. The equivalent of literati in an oral society (bards, priests, leaders) would have been the conservatives of their day, wedded to face-to-face dealings in the high-flown business of government and high-society entertainment. Those of lowlier status had no such inhibitions.

At the centre of Athens, a kilometre north-west of the Acropolis, was the Agora. The word originally meant an assembly, but grew to mean both a town's meeting-place and market-place. Until it was rebuilt in formal style after the Persian Wars in the fifth century BC, the Athenian Agora was a large open space that flowed around a jumble of colonnaded buildings. Here, everything public happened. Priests, politicians and lawyers rubbed shoulders with traders, craftsmen and servants. It is the artisans who concern us, because it was they who not only carried knowledge of the Phoenician letters, but were also keen to use them, as hundreds of graffiti on potsherds and walls reveal. Epigraphers love this stuff. It is raw evidence, left by ordinary people with no thought of history, concerned only about the moment. Their scratchings show the alphabet in the process of formation, as people try different letter shapes and styles. From other fragmentary finds elsewhere, it is even possible to identify where different writers came from. Lines run from left to right, right to left and occasionally in the style known as 'ox-turning', or boustrophedon, because at the end of a line, the letters

,shguolp ti nehw seod xo na sa sevlesmeht no kcab nrut

though no one was quite sure whether, if you did that, the letters should be sbɿɒwʞɔɒd as well, or even ǝpᴉsdn uʍop.

In the Agora, potters, masons and carpenters, using stones and bits of pottery, scratched little ABC exercises to remind themselves of the order of the Phoenician letters. They wrote their names, as tourists scribble 'So and so was here'. They marked their possessions: 'Of Tharrios I am the cup'. They scribbled insults about their mates: 'The boy is lewd', 'Sikela is a lecher'. On a rough pot, someone wrote a parody of the inscriptions on the amphorae given to sporting champions: 'Titas the Olympic victor is a lecherous fellow'. Was this a slander on a virile champion or a dig at a potter's mate with a reputation for bedroom gymnastics? They sent each other messages: 'Eumelis, come as quickly as you can. Abresimos', reads one, and another: 'Boy, bring other new couches for Phalanthos'. They scribbled lists of goods for shopping and meals: 'Kneading-trough, 20 long loaves, 4 middle-sized platters . . .'

One little message can be made to tell a trivial story. It was found in a pit together with two vases, one of which is signed by a certain Thamneos. It seems that this Thamneos borrows a saw from a friend who comes originally from Megara, twenty miles to the west. Both men are craftsmen who have often used Phoenician letters to leave each other notes. The man from Megara is on his way out of Athens. Perhaps a younger brother has come to fetch him because their mother is sick. Anyway, on the road he suddenly remembers the saw. Thamneos will try to return it, and he, the Megaran, won't be at home to receive it. What to do? He remembers there's a safe place to leave the saw, a little storm-drain under the stone that leads into his garden, if only he can tell Thamneos about it. He casts around, finds a broken pot beside the road, chips off the base, picks up a stone and scratches a message. Here, he tells his younger brother, run back and leave this at Thamneos's place, he'll understand. Thamneos finds the message, and reads his friend's letters, slightly oddly formed in the Megaran style: 'Put the saw under the threshold of the garden gate.' OK. He does as he's asked, then throws the message away, along with two of his broken pots, in a little heap that is found 2500 years later.

As part of the process by which the alphabet spread, someone, or many people, turned the oral tales into the epics ascribed to Homer. It was this great work of transcription that kick-started alphabetical literacy in the western world. How and when this happened is not known, and probably never will be, unless some miracle of archaeology turns up early written drafts. In the fifth century, Herodotus claimed that Homer lived 400 years before his time – about 825 BC. Between 750 and 550 BC, oral literature became written literature. At some moment, early in this window, Homer was turned from bard to author. Before then, Homer was in flux, open to retelling at every performance; afterwards he was fixed, frozen as it were in mid-flight; and so his transcribed works became text (though even the written versions varied until an authorized version emerged in the second century BC.)

Perhaps transcription is the wrong word. Imagine that in the intervening four or five hundred years since the Trojan War, as the Greek city-states emerge, a guild of bards forms, singers and reciters who are expert at improvising on the old stories. Between them, they build a collection of tales. By long-established tradition, they use a particular verse form, in which each line is a hexameter, six 'feet' of 13–17 syllables, depending on the number of short and long vowels. Many of the tales would have been self-contained, like Odysseus and the Cyclops. Some bits, now widely separated, could have been made to run together: the opening of the *Iliad* (the quarrel) ends with a prediction of fatal effects, which occur in Book 8. Perhaps bards would have been able, on request, to abstract from the corpus only those tales that involve the gods, a sort of Olympian soap opera. Perhaps originally there was no beginning and no end, but a cycle that could be entered anywhere.

Gradually, a unifying narrative emerges. The bards edit out those tales that conflict, perhaps because the themes are no longer of interest to the evolving society, or because there is no strong theme, or because the chronology is all wrong. Some of them get into the habit of using ostraca, papyrus or parchment to write down opening lines or links between stories, just to remind themselves of what works, even exchanging their notes to compare solutions. Perhaps Homer's greatness lay in taking this whole task in hand, deciding on the sequence of anticipations and confirmations that tie the narrative together. Or perhaps he did little more than provide finishing touches to a process that had been underway for generations.

In any event, some time after the alphabet has become commonplace, there comes a moment. Albert Lord's words about Parry's work with Balkan bards captures what might have happened some 2500 years earlier:

Someone approached the singer and asked him to tell the song so that he could write down the words. In a way this was just one more performance for the singer, one more in a long series. Yet it was the strangest performance he had ever given. There was no music and no song, nothing to keep him to the regular beat except the echo of previous singings and the habit they had formed in his mind. Without these accompaniments it was not easy to put the words together as he usually did. The tempo of composing the song was different, too. Ordinarily the singer could move forward rapidly from idea to idea, from theme to theme. But now he had to stop very often for the scribe to write down what he was saying, after every line or even part of a line. This was difficult, because his mind was far ahead. But he accustomed himself to this new process, and finally the song was finished.

A living thing had been captured, and one world sacrificed to create another.

A performance like that would have been a unique creation, as all performances were. But the transcription of Homer was unique in another sense as well. Other epics have been transcribed, many more since Parry and Lord worked in the Balkans in the 1930s, but always by outsiders who were not raised either with the language or the culture. The recording of Homer was the only occasion known in which those who invented a script also transcribed their own stories.

In this way Homer's oral culture was recorded in something like its full range and splendour, as the oral cultures of Mesopotamia and Egypt (assuming they existed) were not. Even the Bible, written in the consonantal version of the alphabet, lacks the full range of response that characterizes Homer. These texts are ritualized and simplified, acquiring austerity and dignity, but lack the richness that only a single author could impose, and the spontaneity that once came from song.

The change-over from orality to literacy was slow, for there was a convention to be overcome: the oral tradition, preserved by the bards. Poetry still ruled. If poets wrote their works down, it was as an aid to recitation, for an audience, not a readership. The first verse known to have been written by its author was composed by Archilochus of Paros in about 650 BC. The laws of Solon, written either side of 600 BC, were probably inscribed in wood as a record, but they were made public as verse. Inscriptions were made in plenty from the sixth century onwards, but that is no more evidence of general literacy than the massive legal inscriptions that record the laws of the Assyrian ruler, Hammurabi. There was no dulling of oratorical skills, which retained their high status.

Early in the fifth century, Athenian citizens had a chance to write, when they were expected to vote on whether to exile some notoriously dangerous person. The votes were cast by scratching a name on ostraca, those ubiquitous broken bits of pottery that acted as notepaper. Someone who was ejected from the city in this way was 'ostracized'. The existence of ostracism suggests that everyone could write, but a closer look at the scanty evidence suggests this may not have been so. One example concerned Themistocles, the great military leader who in the 480s built the Athenian navy, made peace with Sparta and defeated the Persians in 479 BC. Later, when he argued that Athens and Sparta could not remain in alliance, Athenians turned against him and ostracized him. Of the ostraca 190 survive, but the handwriting on them reveals something odd. They are not the work of 190 different men. Only 14 hands can be identified. Either this was a severe case of ballot rigging; or, more likely, it suggests that even in 473 BC, some 300 years after the introduction of the alphabet, fewer than 10 per cent of its senior citizens trusted themselves to write their own names.

Further support for this view comes from a red-figure vase showing an Athenian school around 480 BC. On it, a teacher displays a Homeric text and another seems to be correcting an essay, images commonly used as evidence that this is a lesson in reading and writing, and that literacy was an important part of Athenian fifth-century schooling. But there is an alternative explanation. In both cases the pupil is standing apart from the teacher, not sitting at a desk as Sumerian schoolboys had to do. It seems that the Athenian boys are being instructed not in reading but in the art of recitation. They know how to read and write, but these are activities still done by lowly artisans, not by the scions of rich citizens. It's more important that these young aristocrats know how to declaim. The Homeric quotations on the drawing are not exact, more like prompts than quotes. And in two other scenes, the boys are being instructed in the lyre and the flute. Music, poetry, recitation: these are the skills required of an upper-class fifth-century Athenian boy, not reading and writing.

For another generation or two, intellectuals retained this patrician attitude towards writing. In his *Phaedrus*, a dialogue between Phaedrus and Socrates, Plato has Socrates quote a pharaoh's condemnation of the god Thoth, inventor of writing: 'If men learn this, it will plant forgetfulness in their souls . . . What you have discovered is a recipe not for memory, but for reminder.' This was not true wisdom, but its semblance. You know, Phaedrus, Socrates continues, written words 'seem to talk to you as though they were intelligent, but if you ask them anything . . . they go on telling you just the same thing forever.' Besides, once something is written down, you never know who might read it. No, for true wisdom, you need human interaction – dialogue – with the right people, lovers of knowledge, like Socrates. And, it went without saying, Plato.

By then, though, this must have been an elitist attitude. Literacy had become widespread. By the end of the fifth century, it seems that most Athenians, or at least its male citizens, read and wrote. Plato referred to 'biblia' – single folded sheets of papyrus – which could be bought for a drachma. The practice of ostracism died out, perhaps because literacy brought in better means of recording opinions. A character in Aristophanes' play *Frogs* makes a passing remark that is the first explicit allusion to literacy: 'As I sat on deck reading the *Andromeda* [of Euripides] to myself . . .' The new alphabetic writing, with its range of vowel sounds, had at last established itself.

For two or three centuries, while the change-over occurred, Greek literature looked both ways, back to an oral past, forward to a literary future. By 550 BC, something wonderful – the urge to memorize and extemporize – was slipping slowly away from the culture. No longer would the collective memory of the Greeks be held in the minds and skills of bards, who wrapped up history, music, morality and much practical knowledge in narrative form.

But other wonders were beginning to emerge. From now on, these cultural features became increasingly uncoupled from each other, and could be pursued as independent subjects. Music separated from words, evolving its own traditions. Freed from the demands of narrative, other themes became specialities. Aristotle's astonishing range of interests were an epitome of them: logic, physics, cosmology, psychology, metaphysics, theology, ethics, politics, rhetoric, poetry, biology. Previously history had been embedded in Homeric narrative. Now, Herodotus and Thucydides became the first 'modern' historians, attempting to use objective evidence to record and explain events. Justice, once a balancing of behaviour, status, religion and desire, could now become a matter for courts, with written laws and precedents. That we're all democrats at last is thanks to the Athenians. (You may say they weren't really democrats because they excluded women, resident aliens and slaves, but what Athens lacked in theory it made up for in practice. For a century and a half, democracy was a duty and a passion, which involved as high a proportion of Athens's population as of today's vast and apathetic electorates.)

A new mode of thought became possible, or at least many times easier. For the first time, thinkers could generalize, with a purpose. It is hard, when composing or listening to narrative, to hold generalities in mind for long. They have to be very tightly packaged if they are not to disturb the narrative and send the heavier drinkers to sleep. Now, though, writers produce statements independent of character and action, without an Agamemnon or an Achilles or a quarrel to anchor them. Consider one of the most famous of generalizations, Aristotle's conclusion that 'Mankind is by nature a political animal.' Of all the things to be said about this statement, two are relevant here. Firstly, Hollywood it definitely ain't. This is not the stuff of narrative. We are into the realm of pure thought, considering a great truth about all human beings. But secondly, it is the product of a chain of evidence and logic which, when opened up, invites endless argument ('A *political* animal?' – but surely Aristotle was merely reflecting his own life-style, that of a man who lived in a *polis*? – so is he saying that we are all communal by nature? – or 'city-creatures'? – or that we *should* be? – and where does that leave tribesmen, villagers and citizens of empires?). It would have been very hard to hold in mind a non-narrative conclusion like this, with its chains of arguments, without the backup provided by an accessible, easily learned script.

This fascination for the general, the factual and the analytical produced extremely powerful intellectual tools, which then fed back to create extraordinary practical consequences. It is an astonishing leap from the practical concerns of Sumerians and Egyptians, from the creation of drainage channels, ziggurats and pyramids, to the unphysical qualities of shapes that do not exist in the real world. When Archimedes tried to pin down π or Pythagoras saw the hidden nature of right-angled triangles, the shapes were not physical, because any real-life circle or triangle would be coarse and unreliable impressions of the '*realer*' ones, the mental constructs.

With the alphabet to hand, knowledge piled on knowledge as never before, as one chain of causes and effects reveals. Aristotle passed his famous school, the Lyceum, to his successor Theophrastus. Both taught Alexander the Great, who collected books by the thousand. Alexander founded Alexandria in Egypt (the greatest of no less than fifty Alexandrias), and commanded that it should have a great library, in the tradition of great rulers. When one of his generals, Ptolemy, made Alexandria the capital of Egypt, he commissioned Demetrius, a former ruler of Athens and also a student of Aristotle, to create the library as the city's central feature. It became the greatest in the ancient world, a research centre into which would flow everything ever written, either the original or a copy. Library, museum and shrine all in one, it gathered works on mathematics, philosophy, government, history and the arts. It had a garden, a zoo and an observatory. Its scholars organized games, festivals and literary competitions. In its cloisters and porticoed wings – though no one actually knows what it looked like – up to a hundred scholars at a time could work. Here Archimedes researched the 'screw' that bears his name, the geographer Eratosthenes advised that it would be possible to reach India by way of Spain, and Aristarchos claimed that the Earth went round the Sun. Scribes translated hieroglyphic and cuneiform texts. Passing ships were boarded by officials who seized any books aboard for copying. The library had, so it was said, half a million scrolls and codices. Gradually, though, history started to pass Alexandria by. The library's reputation fell. It burned down in the late third century AD, and three centuries later its remains finally fell into the hands of the Arabs when they invaded in 641. The conqueror Amrou Ibn el-As knew his duty: if the few surviving scrolls conformed with the Koran's teachings, Muslims had no need of them; if they didn't, there was no need to preserve them. 'Proceed, then,' he said, 'and destroy them.'

Long before that moment, Greek literary creations had become part of the world's intellectual patrimony, thanks to our imaginary scholar, the adapter of the alphabet. Already by the time of the library's formation, this restless invention was seeking new lands, and new peoples, with open minds and a drive to match that of the ancient Greeks.

9

WHY WE DON'T WRITE ETRUSCAN

C entral Italy in the eighth century BC was a colonist's dream, a land of reed-roofed houses and Iron Age farmers, with no power-ful cities, palaces, citadels, or temples, or stone buildings of any kind, as far as archaeologists can tell. The Phoenicians in their surge westwards showed little interest in Italy, being more concerned to set up ports and trading stations, like Carthage and Utica on the north African coast, looking across the 100-mile strait to other bases on the tip of Sicily. But the Greeks, when they started thrusting outwards in the early 800s, had a different agenda. They wanted land. Once the Aegean and mainland were occupied, they found their eastern approaches were blocked by Phoenicians and

Assyrians. Westwards lay Italy, and land that must have seemed ripe for the plucking. In about 770 BC, settlers from Euboea made a toe-hold off Naples, on Pithekoussai, the island on which Nestor's cup found its final resting place. This was not an ideal base, with its unreliable volcano and a few Phoenicians already in residence. Greeks spread ashore soon afterwards, to more fertile land around Cumae, and then to a score of other bases around the coasts of Sicily and the Italian south. Too late, the Phoenicians saw what was at risk, and staked out their own new settlements, in Sardinia and the Balearics, starting a long-standing rivalry for trading posts, bases and raw materials.

Amidst this slowly evolving struggle, there arose a third people, totally different from the two major participants, a people who were to have an astonishing impact on their homeland. They were the Etruscans, who became Italy's first city-dwellers, with art, architecture, social structures and an alphabet that might have given them a literature to rival that of the Greeks. In establishing their empire of city-states, they reached out south of the Tiber, into barbaric Latium, and developed another, greater city. Worse luck for them, for its Latin citizens took care to appropriate Etruscan culture, alphabet and all, so completely that they were able to bury the memory of their founders and their language in myth, leaving an echo of Etruria only in place names, in massive stonework and tombs by the tens of thousands.

It was not Romulus who founded Rome, not its inhabitants who introduced the alphabet to Europe's future rulers. It was the Etruscans, long lost, and still in the process of resurrection.

Thomas Dempster, scholar and hooligan, has been pretty much forgotten. He rates no mention in a modern *Britannica*. But his fame and infamy increase in retrospect. The 1911 *Britannica* gave him a full column. In his own time, that of Shakespeare, this brilliant, vain, pugnacious Scot was admired and reviled across western Europe. By the time he died in Italy, he had completed seven erudite volumes which explain his inclusion here, because they summarized everything then known about the mysterious people through whom the alphabet jumped from Greece to Rome. He has some claim to be the father of Etruscology.

By his own account, Dempster was extraordinary from the moment of his birth in 1579. The twenty-fourth of twenty-nine children, and one of triplets, he claimed to have learned the alphabet in a single hour when he was three. His home life was as violent as Macbeth's – an elder brother James married his father's mistress, provoking a family feud that forced James to flee to Holland. There, after brawling with an officer, he was executed by being tied to four horses, which were spurred off in different directions and tore James to bits. Even as a teenager, Thomas was someone to be reckoned with: tall, with jet-black hair, 'his bodily aspect altogether kingly; his strength and courage equal to that of any soldier'. Taking advantage of the Scottish Catholics' dangerous links with France, he was educated in Paris, Rome and Douai, where he wrote such a scurrilous attack on Elizabeth I that it caused the English students to riot, the first revelation of those explosive combinations – impetuousness and brilliance, bombast and scholarship – that define his whole restless life, and turn an account of it into a mantra of fights and flights. Still a teenager, he lectured in Tournai, took a law degree in Paris, then taught in Toulouse until he was thrown out after a row. Elected professor of rhetoric in Nîmes, he fought an embittered rival for the post, was sued for libel, and fled. A tutorship in Spain ended in similar fashion. Back in Scotland, an argument with the clergy drove him back to France. Numerous teaching posts led to Beauvais, where he sparked his nastiest brawl yet. After a duel with a young officer, he had the man held, stripped and buggered in public by a 'lusty fellow'. When three of the victim's friends – officers of the king's horse guards, no less – came for revenge, Dempster, at the head of a troop of college staff, penned the officers in a belfry and kept them there for several days. That ended his time in Beauvais.

Somehow he had found time to write as well as teach and fight. In 1615, a book dedicated to James I won him an invitation to the English court, where Anglican clergy opposed royal patronage of this disputatious Catholic. Before heading back to Paris, he married. He was thirty-six, still in his compelling prime, when he won the affections of Susanna Valeria, a girl so astoundingly beautiful and provocative that she caused Parisians to riot. According to the encylopaedist, Pierre Bayle, writing towards the end of the century, when she appeared with her husband in the streets, 'in a most enchanting dress, exposing to public view a neck and breast whiter than the purest snow, such a crowd of people flocked from all sides to see her, that, had they not taken flight in a neighbouring house, it is more than probable they would have been crushed to death'.

Moving swiftly on, this time to Rome, Dempster won backing from the pope, through whose influence with Cosimo, grand duke of Tuscany, he was made Professor of Civil Law in the University of Pisa. And it was here that in 1616–19, he wrote the books for which Etruscologists remember him. *De Etruria Regali Libri Septem* (Seven Books Concerning the Kingdom of Etruria) gathers virtually everything then known about the origin, customs, history, conquests and government of the Etruscans. After he presented the manuscript to his sponsor, Cosimo, Pope Urban VIII gave him a pension. Fame, of the right sort, was his; but as usual infamy was not far behind. Susanna, becoming bored perhaps with his habit of reading for 14 hours a day, eloped with an English student. Dempster set off in furious pursuit. It was summer, and Tuscany was notoriously malarial. He died of fever in Bologna on 6 September.

Cosimo shelved Dempster's manuscript on the Etruscans. But when it was finally published a century later, in 1723, it founded a national, then an international, vogue for all things Etruscan: murals, bronzes, statues, pottery, inscriptions that no one understood. In the days before archaeology, a vogue meant profit for landowners, work for peasants, fashionable collections for those who could pay, and the destruction of what remained of a priceless heritage. One landowner was Lucien Bonaparte, brother of Napoleon, who sold off 2000 Etruscan artefacts dug from just four acres of his estate in the 1820s. Tombs by the tens of thousand were torn open and emptied. In one excavation at Vulci in 1843, the British Etruscologist, George Dennis, watched helpless as an overseer ordered the smashing of anything that might not sell on the antique market. 'Labourers crushed them beneath their feet as things "cheaper than seaweed". In vain we pleaded to save some from destruction; they were *roba di sciocchezza* ("foolish stuff").' The tomb was then filled in and ploughed over. It was from private collections, formed from such depredation, that great museums built their own collections. And these collections represent the merest fraction of what once existed in the ground, itself a fraction of the remnants of a rich, civilized and attractive people to whom Romans and all Europe owe more than most care to acknowledge.

Despite the mass of material, the language of the Etruscans remained as mysterious as their origins. All of the inscriptions were short, none except the most rudimentary of them bilingual. So even the first extended text went unrecognized, its nature emerging by chance long after its discovery.

In the mid-nineteenth century, European demand fuelled a lucrative trade in Egyptian coffins and their mummified contents stolen from pharaonic tombs. Tourists were often fobbed off with sawdust and animal bones bandaged up with rags. In 1848, Michael Baric, a Croatian official in the Austro-Hungarian chancellery in Alexandria and an amateur Egyptologist, bought a sarcophagus, which turned out to contain a genuine mummy. He took it home and for the next ten years kept it standing in the corner of his drawing room, telling visitors that it was the sister of Hungary's founder, King Stephen. When he died, his brother gave the mummy to the Zagreb Museum, where its bandages were removed. To the astonishment of the staff, they found that the linen strips were covered in strange writing 'in an unknown and hitherto undeciphered language'. They were examined by a leading German Egyptologist, Heinrich Brugsch, who was baffled.

There matters rested until the adventurer, explorer and author, Richard Burton, happened to meet up with Brugsch in Egypt in 1877. Burton, a living legend for his bitterly disputed discovery of the source of the Nile, was then British consul in Trieste. In one of his many scholarly roles, he was researching runic letters, a northern European alphabet that existed for over 1500 years. Brugsch told him of the Zagreb Mummy: 'Imagine my surprise when I found that the characters were not hieroglyphs, but partly Graeco-Roman and partly Runic.' Burton was intrigued. He sent a note asking the local British vice-consul in Zagreb for help.

The vice-consul, Philip Cautley, called on the museum's director early in 1878, thus becoming the first to trace part of one of the two extended texts in Etruscan. Not that he recognized it. Nor did Burton, though Burton himself had written on Etruscan artefacts. Nor did anyone else. When Burton published the extract in 1882 in the *Transactions of the Royal Society of Literature*, the discovery was ignored, until research on the bandages themselves in Vienna in the 1890s revealed the script for what it was.

Why would an Egyptian mummy be wrapped in linen scribbled on by an Etruscan? The Austrian researcher, Jakob Krall, turned detective. The writing was on the inner surface, against the mummy's skin, so it was clearly not meant to be on show. Moreover the strips had been torn randomly, and the lines were mixed up.

In brief, there was no necessary connection between mummy and wrapping – unless the girl was an Etruscan whose family had fled to Egypt after the Roman take-over. But in that case, surely the wrappings would have had significance, and not been treated so haphazardly? Experts prefer to assume that the girl was Egyptian and that the wrappings were to hand by chance, discarded presumably by Etruscan refugees.

The Zagreb Mummy began to recall the Etruscans from their limbo. But the challenge had a unique twist. Usually, if a dead language is incomprehensible, it is because it cannot be read. If it can be read, especially if it had close contacts with nearby cultures, it should be comprehensible. But Etruscan isn't. It is of an entirely different language group from anything in the area; in fact, it has no known relatives. With no links or any bilingual text, meaning is absent. The 1200-word text, made up of some 500 different words, since there are many repetitions, can be read easily enough, because it, like other Etruscan inscriptions, is written in easily learned Graeco-Phoenician letters. Some 13,000 inscriptions are now known, most of them short, most of them carved on tombs, funeral urns and sarcophagi, all written in letters familiar from Phoenician and Greek. There are names in plenty, some obviously familiar: Aplu (Apollo), Hercle (Hercules), Alexsantre (Alexander). Brief bilingual inscriptions and references by Greek writers have now provided a vocabulary of 1000 or so words, of which only about 100 have universally agreed meanings, with the merest hints of grammar.

The mystery is an invitation to eccentrics. There has been, and is, a steady stream of would-be translations, most categorically self-confident, based on assumptions that Etruscan is derived from any number of languages, including Basque, Old Norse, Celtic, Tuareg and Malay. Take one incantation in the so-called Book of the Mummy of Zagreb, as the linen scroll is known:

>*Ceia hia*
>*Etnam ciz vacl trin vale*

One French translator, an eminent professor who decided that Finnish was the key to Etruscan, insisted this meant 'Shout! With force! Now the response – very loudly, raise the voice! Attention!' Another, convinced that Etruscan had Egyptian roots, suggested a somewhat different version: 'The fire has thrown its rays, Come and distribute food.' Others, equally bizarre and assured, include a Nordic-based version: 'Stride with frenzy, bewitch the banquet, three times upset . . .' and an Albanian one: 'Call the shades, call the shades to the fathers, live again . . .'

If Etruscans ever wrote their own history, and did so bilingually, their works were destroyed or have still to emerge. In the search for Etruscan origins, experts must make do with inferences drawn from archaeology, works of art, myth, and hints from Greek and Roman authors.

Herodotus, writing in the fifth century BC, when the Etruscans had been masters of central Italy for over two centuries, says they came from Lydia in western Turkey, famous for its capital, Sardis, and for Croesus, its proverbially wealthy king. According to Herodotus, Lydia was struck by a famine so intense that half its population emigrated under a legendary prince, Tyrrhennos (the root-name of Etruria, Etruscan, Toscana and Tuscany, as well as the name of the Mediterranean off Naples). They marched west to Smyrna, built a fleet and sailed away beyond Greece to found a new homeland in Italy. Those who wish to believe this (and many archaeologists now discount it) argue in its favour from vague evidence – the dice-games that Etruscans and Lydians both played, the similarities between Lydian and Etruscan tombs and effigies, the joint love of flute music, a shared pantheon of gods and goddesses. Thucydides mentions Tyrrhenians coming from the northern Aegean island of Lemnos, where a grave stele was found inscribed with letters that may be Etruscan. But the stele seems to postdate the Etruscans' supposed arrival in Italy. Perhaps later Etruscan travellers buried one of their fellows there, and so started the story of a link. At present, the only certainty is that, from the evidence of graves, the Etruscans were in Italy by about 750 BC. Fifty years later, the graves had become monumental, as they would remain for centuries – rooms, solid as houses, with primitive vaults, circular walls of rock, whole villages of graves, with grave goods recalling the wealth and sophistication of a culture already known well enough to the Greeks to be mentioned by Homer.

By then, the Etruscans were building their first city-states. Fields were planted, forests cleared, swamps drained. Towns arose, not yet with the massive stone walls that typified them later, for there were no enemies yet. To the south they founded Caere and Veii, near present-day Rome; to the north, Tarquinii, which the Etruscans thought of as their foundation city, Vetluna, Rusellae, Pupluna, Valethri (modern Volterra), and Camars, which the Romans called Clusium and today's Italians know as Chiusi. Further inland there followed Arezzo, Perugia and Cortona, whose towering walls and stone carapace would still be familiar to a resurrected Etruscan. Paved roads joined the towns. Ports received ships with ivory, scarabs and ostrich eggs from Africa, incense from Arabia, cauldrons from Anatolia, oil, perfumes and pottery from Greece. Potters turned out beautiful glossy black jars, decorated with mythical figures taken from Egypt and Mesopotamia. The Etruscans cultivated – perhaps even introduced – grapes for wine and made wonderful ewes-milk pecorino. They knew about drains, and city water supplies, and built superb aqueducts. They were great metal workers. Outside Pupluna, huge rusty mounds turned out last century to be slag heaps so rich in iron that the Italians mined them to make artillery shells during the First World War. They loved music: the Etruscan flute-players were virtuosi who, it was said, could pipe wild animals into snares, and the Etruscan war-trumpet was adopted by the Romans as their *tuba*. Murals in the Greek style decorated the tombs of the rich and life-sized terracotta statues adorned roofs and sarcophagi. A particular style of architecture emerged, with an entrance-hall, or *atrium*, originally an Etruscan word for 'entrance'. To the Etruscans, Europe owes an ominous debt: the symbol of royal authority was an axe bound with rods, which, when inherited by the Romans, became known as a *fascis* (bundle), and which 2500 years later was seized upon by Mussolini as the symbol and name for his Fascists.

Then there is the alphabet. A people migrating from Turkey westwards through the Aegean in Homer's time could possibly have picked it up en route, from Phoenicians or Greeks. Some have seen significance in the fact that the Lydian and Etruscan alphabets shared a new letter, an *f* which looked like a figure 8. But the Lydian alphabet, known from only a hundred or so examples, is later than the earliest Etruscan one: it and its *f/8* could have been carried in the opposite direction. If there is any truth in the migration story, it seems unlikely that writing would have been foremost in Etruscan minds until they had a secure base, and towns, and an economy, and wealth enough to make monuments that needed inscriptions. Whether Etruscans were immigrants or indigenous, by about 700 BC, this metal-rich culture – with all the youth and ambition that would have inspired the invention or adoption of a script – had a source of literacy close to hand: Greek colonists from Euboea who had been on the island of Ischia and Cumae for two or three generations. Ischia and Cumae were just 120 miles south of the Etruscans' southern borders.

On the plain ten miles inland from Orbetello, beside a large river, is the village of Marsiliana. In the seventh century BC, this was a fine place to live, on a hilly plateau that is a natural fortress, overlooking fertile fields watered by a navigable river, the Albegna. For some two hundred years, Marsiliana prospered. Its wealth is reflected in its hundred or so rich tombs, dug into gravel beneath overhanging layers of hard limestone known as travertine or trenched graves surrounded by large travertine slabs. One, known as the Circle of the Ivories, was packed with gold jewellery and bronzes as well as ivory objects, which date it to about 625 BC. Though most of the items were imported from as far away as Mesopotamia, several little ivories must have been carved locally, for they include dog-like animals with wavy manes – lions, by a sculptor who had never seen one.

Among the objects was one of special interest. It is a minute rectangular tablet just 8cm (a little over 3 inches) long, with a raised border and a holder of some sort at one end. Tablets of this shape were common enough in

Greece and Phoenicia. Filled with a thin layer of wax, they were used to scribble on with a pointed stylus. A few drops of new wax renewed the surface. But this thing was too small to be practical. Yet across the top, from right to left, runs a Greek alphabet, all twenty-six letters. What was it doing in the tomb? The best explanation is that it belonged to a rich and accomplished man. He knew the alphabet, but could do with the odd reminder, so he used to wear this toy writing tablet strung round his neck as proof of his learning and his links with the sophisticated east, and as a ready-reference. When he died (not long before his town was destroyed) this adornment was buried with him.

Other finds show how widespread knowledge of the Graeco-Phoenician alphabet became. Those funerary inscriptions list thousands of names. Jugs record their owners, and ink-pots act as memo pads for alphabets. One was in the shape of a cockerel, made around 600 BC, with an alphabet written around it to remind the writer of the letters: in this case, the twenty-two letters of the Phoenician alphabet with the four Greek additions;

Later, the Etruscans dropped *b, d, g* and *o*. The *8 (f)* symbol came later, leaving a mature alphabet of twenty-three letters, based not on the classical Greek forms but variants developed by their Euboean neighbours on Ischia.

How this alphabet came to be Roman involves the story of how one culture fell and the other rose.

It is a truism of historical teaching that the Romans founded Rome. Schoolchildren are taught the story to this day of how Romulus founded the Eternal City on the Palatine Hill in 753 BC, the date *ab urbe condita* (from the foundation of the city) which Romans accepted as their historical baseline. The date was calculated by the historian Varro in the first century BC and the story was edited together by Livy a generation later. But Livy did not pretend to be telling the literal truth. The old tales he said 'had more the charm of poetry than of a sound historical record . . . There is no reason, I feel, to object when antiquity draws no hard line between the human and the supernatural; it adds dignity to the past.'

Archaeological research this century has provided what Livy could not: an account of Rome's origins that dignifies not the Romans but the Etruscans. The hills of Rome had been settled for millennia when, in the eighth century, Latin tribesmen built several villages of wattle-and-daub huts on hills, gradually spreading into those valleys which were not turned into malarial marshes by the Tiber's floods. Around 700 BC the Etruscans were drawn to the area by a ford across the river and the flood-free hills. It was a good spot for expansion: far enough inland for the river to be bridged, close enough to the coast for seagoing ships. A broken pot bearing the letters 'UQNUS' dates from this time. It is Rome's earliest inscription: Etruscan, not Roman. A little later the remains are of pots made in nearby Caere and Veii – all Etruscan. Two princely tombs, founded in 1855 and 1876 in Praeneste, a few miles south-east of Rome, show that the Etruscans were already penetrating these wilder regions peacefully in the early seventh century. A couple of generations later, in about 625 BC, the first stonework appeared and under Etruscan guidance Latin huts gave way to the beginnings of an Etruscan city. They called it Rumlua, which became Romulus, which, like Kadmos and perhaps Tyrrhenos, was turned into a man, and cloaked with legendary origins and spurious successors.

Rome's first historical king, Lucomo, was no Roman. He came from Tarquinii, the Etruscans' main city. He and his young wife chose to make a life on the frontier, with its scattering of villages and illiterate tribesmen. Once established, he took a new name, Tarquinius Priscus, recalling his home town. By about 607, he had made himself ruler, securing his position by acting as defender against neighbouring Latin tribes and as Rome's first architect. Funded by loot from campaigns into surrounding tribal areas, Etruscan engineers built drains, cleared the marsh between the Capitol and the Palatine hills, covered a side stream in a stone tunnel, and built in sun-baked brick on proper foundations. About 575 BC, as archaeological strata reveal, the wattle huts with their straw and reed roofs were flattened, and their remains covered in a hardcore of pebbles, forming a huge open space at the foot of the Palatine: the Forum, the future centre of the Roman Empire.

Tarquin's success brought a challenge, in the form of an invasion by a certain Etruscan named Mastarna, who invaded and seized power and renamed himself Servius Tullius. In forty years, he accomplished a social revolution, introducing taxation, surveys of property, a census, and a legal system, all underpinning an army of unprecedented size and power. Rome became a city-state under arms, with every citizen allotted to a hundred-strong regiment – a 'century', under its own commander, a centurion.

It was this system that was taken over, with tyrannical force, by Tarquin's grandson, Tarquinius Superbus, Tarquin the Proud. The new town grew. In a half-mile valley between the Palentine and Aventine hills, the Circus Maximus took shape. Tarquin knew what he wanted: a mural in Tarquinii shows an Etruscan funerary games, with sprinters, boxers, javelin-throwers and charioteers in action. Horses and sportsmen brought in from Etruria provided the first games, the start of a millennium of Roman entertainments. A great wooden temple to Tinia, the Etruscan Jupiter, arose on the Capitoline Hill, a building to rival even the rebuilt temple of Solomon in Jerusalem. A Great Sewer – the Cloaca Maxima – ran for 600 yards from the Forum to the Tiber (some of it still survives). Tarquin built on his grandfather's vision, dressing in purple, wearing a golden crown on ceremonial occasions, when he was flanked by twelve attendant lictors, each bearing the axe and bundle of rods, symbolic of Etruria's twelve main cities.

Rome became one of Etruria's major cities. Etruscan rule spread south, across Campania, threatening the Greek colony, Cumae, and thus becoming a major player in Mediterranean intercultural politics. In about 600, Greek colonists settled in the south of France, at Massalia (now Marseilles). These Phocaeans, from present-day Foca on the west coast of Turkey, had been chased out when Persia rose to power. Their arrival was a spark in a powder keg, for they could monopolize the trade in tin which came down the Rhône from Britain. Phoenicians in Carthage took exception. So did the Etruscans, who saw a threat to their coastal trade and their contacts with Phoenicians and the Aegean. When in 545 the Greeks invaded Corsica, the Etruscans took action. Etruria allied with Carthage, formed a naval force of 120 ships, and defeated the Greeks off their Corsican base, Alalia, in one of the earliest and most significant of Mediterranean sea battles.

Now secure, the Etruscans reached out further. By 550 BC they dominated central Italy from present-day Pisa to Naples. An Etruscan road wound over the 3000-ft Passo della Colline towards Florence. In about 500 BC, outside Bologna, near the village of Marzobotto, they built a city, Misa; its gridiron street plan, with houses, workshops, an acropolis and two temples, is on view today. Piacenza, Modena, Mantua, Ravenna: they were all Etruscan foundations. An Etruscan town which guarded the Po – its flood-prone mouth controlled by Etruscan hydraulic engineers – was called Atria ('entrance', the same word as their architectural feature, the *atrium*), which gave its name to the Adriatic. Traders ventured into the foothills of the Alps and beyond. Northern Europe was open. Celtic chieftains scooped Etruscan wine from Etruscan bronze cauldrons with Etruscan flagons.

And everywhere they went they took their alphabet. German tribes north of the Alps must have been aware of it. Some scholars argue on scanty evidence that they adapted it, and that it was some enterprising German who made up the alphabet later known as Runic, an alphabet that spread north along trade routes, from the Danube, to Scandinavia and to England. What a chance Burton missed by not pursuing his interest in the Zagreb Mummy! The Runic alphabet has its own story, for it remained a declining alternative to the other, Roman heir to the Etruscan alphabet until it died out in remote parts of Sweden in the seventeenth century.

All of this raises a problem. If the Etruscans were so successful, if they dominated the Latin tribes, if they had their own writing system, why is Roman culture not Etruscan? Why do we not write with Etruscan, rather than Roman letters? How come the Latins managed to reverse the position, sweep away Etruria and Etruscan and hijack the writing? It might so easily have gone the other way – an Etruscan empire, leading to Etruscan writing across all Europe, and thus the world.

The answers lie in the way that fate, history, the gods, turned against their once-favoured children.

As every schoolboy used to know, Rome turned republican in 509 BC and threw Tarquin out. A cursory glance at Roman history suggests a popular Latin revolt against Etruscan tyranny. In fact, the revolt was by Etruscan aristocrats, who retained the two highest offices, the consulates, under the new constitution. All the Etruscan trappings remained: crowns, sceptres, ivory thrones, purple-bordered robes, lictors' rods. The exiled Tarquin wanted his town back and led other Etruscan cities into war. An army led by Lars Porsena of Clusium was not balked by Horatius cutting the only wooden bridge across the Tiber – Macaulay's dramatic poem was only the latest retelling of a popular legend. Porsena actually won, by siege, leaving a legacy of bitterness that threatened to cut northern Etruria from its southern half.

Etruria's strength and charm was also its weakness. It consisted of proud and independent city-states who could not combine for long. Their empire had been one less of conquest than of trade and culture. The attempt to gain by force what had been theirs by peaceful means proved their undoing. Though Etruscan leaders remained dominant in Rome for another fifty years, the Romans themselves – the ordinary people who had been colonized by the enterprising Etruscans – asserted their own new-found prosperity and power with a most un-Etruscan austerity. If they read and wrote, they did so in their own language, Latin. They had little interest in Etruscan arts, crafts and commerce, and were scandalized by their neighbours' sumptuous revels. Unlike the Etruscans, the Romans banned women from banquets, and from drinking. Pliny mentions the case of a husband who killed his wife when he found her taking a drink of wine, and was exonerated of murder. The main lesson the Romans learned from the Etruscans was that taught by their first Etruscan rulers: military might paid off. Rome became a barracks, frowning on luxury, refusing imports from Greece, dressing in homespun, eating porridge. The sports ground, the Field of Mars, became a parade ground.

And on the wider stage, too, events turned against the Etruscans. In 482, a Greek naval station closed the Straits of Messina. In 480, their allies, the Carthaginians, suffered a crushing defeat at Himera – hundreds of ships lost and 30,000 killed – when they tried to drive the Greeks from Sicily. Six years later, a joint Etruscan–Carthaginian assault on Cumae ended in disaster when Greeks from Syracuse came to Cumae's help. An Etruscan helmet in the British Museum recalls their defeat. It was a trophy handed to the Greek leader, Hieron, who had it engraved in Greek and took it as a gift to the temple in Olympia. It reads: 'Hieron, son of Deinomenes, and the Syracusans dedicated to Zeus the Etruscan spoils won at Cumae.' Worse, Hieron was given Ischia as a prize. Now all Campania, the Etruscan south, was under threat by sea, just as its northern approaches were cut off by embittered Latins. In 453, sixty Greek triremes raked the Etruscan ports. In Campania, Latin tribesmen swarmed down from the mountains. Pompeii and Capua acquired massive walls, in vain. Etruscan cities, relying now on mercenaries, fell one by one. In 425 BC, Campania was a spent force. In 415, during the Peloponnesian War, the great Greek civil war of 431–404, a joint Etruscan–Athenian attack on Syracuse ended in another disaster: 53 Etruscan ships lost, 7000 Athenians enslaved.

To cut a century's decline short, from Rome's opposition came war, in which the Romans proved merciless. In 396, after a decade of war against the chief remaining Etruscan city, Veii, besiegers infiltrated the town through the Etruscans' famous drains and sewers, and wrenched open the doors. 'A fearful din arose,' Livy recorded. 'Yells of triumph, shrieks of terror, and the pitiful crying of children. Next day all the free-born townsfolk were sold into slavery.' The invaders sacked the town, stripped the temple, and carted off its statue of Juno to Rome. In 354–1, the Romans broke Tarquinii, scorched its lands, enslaved and executed its people, shattered its irrigation works, burned its workshops. Celts attacked in the north, Greeks in the south. A brief revival of spirit was broken by 300 BC. On the walls of Etruscan tombs, the dead no longer smiled, and dancers gave way to demons. When the last independent Etruscan city, Volsinii, fell in 264, it was razed, every house and wall levelled to the ground, its very site forgotten. Rome was free to turn against another ancient enemy, Carthage. By the first century BC, the Etruscan language was dead, perhaps beyond recall.

With the coming of Latin power, the great suppression and the great denial started. Romans scoured tombs for antiques. D. H. Lawrence, who visited Etruria in the 1920s, gave a writer's impression of what must have happened. 'Even when all the gold and silver and jewels had been pilfered from the urns . . . still the vases and the bronzes must have remained in their places. Then the rich Romans began to collect vases, "Greek" vases with the painted scenes. So these were stolen from the tombs. Then the little bronze figures, statuettes, animals and bronze ships, of which the Etruscans put thousands in their tombs, became the rage with Roman collectors.' Not everyone indulged. In the first century BC, the emperor Claudius, whose first wife was part-Etruscan, wrote a twenty-volume history of her people; but it vanished, by mischance or suppression. The Romans owed their very existence to the Etruscans, and obliterated them, perhaps from ordinary greed, perhaps to hide a truth too degrading to admit. In their stories, their origins became their own, or Greek. Etruria became an appendix of Roman history.

The Romans were good, though, at fighting and administering, and for that they needed writing. The Etruscan legacy of letters served them well, with minor adaptations. One involved a re-shuffling of the sounds and forms of *g, c* and *k*. These sounds and letter-forms have their own specialist histories, but the main result was to use the Etruscans' *C*-shape to form a *G*. Other Greek letters – *th*(θ), *ks*(ξ), *kh*(χ), *ps*(ψ) and long *o* had no place in Latin. The Romans dropped the Greek *ph*(φ) but, at the suggestion of the scholar–emperor Claudius, reintroduced the sound as our 'F', basing it on a local, ancient Greek letter, the digamma, which, as an added confusion, had been pronounced as *w* before it fell from use. Finally, the Romans dropped *Υ* and *Z*, then added them back in again, placing them at the end of the line. The end result was an alphabet the same as ours, except without *J, U* or *W*.

These were the twenty-three letters that the Romans made their own, and ours. The key to success was political power, which is reflected in the design of the letters in Roman inscriptions. Naturally, as admirers of all things Greek, they took their lead from the Greeks, who had developed letter-shapes that seemed to exude power and authority. This impression comes from a fine balance between two competing traits, simplicity and decoration. The simplicity lies in thin, equal lines and a uniform squareness; the decoration – a discrete display of a ruler's investment in artistry – is present in the beginnings of those little exaggerations at the end of a stroke that would one day be called serifs. Roman leaders and sculptors took these ideas further, with four-square lettering and smart serifs enriched by variations in the thickness of the strokes. Set in stone under good, strong sunlight, this lettering gives just the right impression. As Stanley Morison, a historian of typefaces and the greatest of modern typeface designers, wrote, the designers and sculptors of the finest Roman inscriptions well understood how to fulfil their task: 'to impress the citizens of conquered provinces'. Whatever the inscriptions said and wherever they stood, their hidden message was symbolized by the letters held aloft on Roman standards: *SPQR – Senatus Populusque Romanus*, 'The Roman Senate and People'. In brief, Rome rules.

And still does in a sense, for their monumental letter-shapes, sanctified anew by the Italian Renaissance, were so admired by Morison that he used them as the basis of the typeface he designed for the London *Times* in the 1930s. Times New Roman, probably the world's most popular typeface, harks straight back to the inscriptions of Augustus and Trajan, whose craftsmen, in Morison's words, 'achieved a height of excellence that has won recognition, universal in the West, as the unsurpassable rendition of the Latin alphabet'.

This broad river of literacy has countless backwaters and tributaries. From early in the history of the Roman empire, the story of the western alphabet merges into other specialist areas of scripts and literacy. Roman lettering spun off other forms, especially after Constantine, the first Christian emperor, turned Rome away from its anti-Christian past. A distinction arose between capital and small letters, majuscule and minuscule. Writing styles by the dozen came and went. But neither the idea nor the fundamental form needed anything but minor tinkering. Only later, in the Middle Ages, would the alphabet be further modified, when V produced both U and, later still, W, which still retains its origins in its name a 'double U' in English, a 'double V' in French. Finally, quite slowly from the fourteenth to seventeenth centuries, I split into two, with a longer, initial variant becoming our modern J.

In effect, soon after Rome became Roman, the Latin alphabet was established, the basic tool that would be carried across Europe. Only eastwards beyond the borders of the empire, were there peoples so remote and barbarous that they remained without a script.

10

THE LIMITS TO GROWTH

_____

This book has looked at the moments at which the emerging alphabet leaped from culture to culture, growing into the most efficient and convenient form of written communication yet devised. Why then, if the western alphabet is so wonderful, is it not even more widely used? The conservatism of established systems points to one set of answers. But not in Europe. Here, the Roman alphabet might have spread from the Atlantic to the Urals, and beyond to the Pacific. In fact, it was blocked by the emergence of a second script, creating a split over a thousand years ago that still divides Europe. The split started, unfortunately, in the Balkans, where tribes, regions and nations tumble through time like a shower of asteroids, interacting unpredictably with themselves and the pull of great planets – Rome and Byzantium, Christianity and Orthodoxy, the Soviet empire and western Europe and Turkey and . . . Even to evoke the complexities makes the mind reel.

One strand, though, can be traced to its roots: the emergence of the script that rivalled and limited the Roman system. Like live things, these two alphabets seemed to seek outlets in borderland cultures. Recently, one new culture has emerged – the Internet – in which the Roman system has already become entrenched. It is possible, though not inevitable, that the Roman alphabet will be universal.

In the ninth century, what remained of the Roman empire was in the process of partition, between a western section that still looked to Rome for its moral authority and its eastern counterpart, Constantinople.

In both, a duarchy of church and state claimed the mantle of Christian authority. Rome was St Peter's city. Constantinople was the capital of the man who brought Christianity to Roman Europe and renamed the city, formerly Byzantium, after himself: Contantine-polis, Constantine's city. Both pope and emperor believed himself to be the true conduit for Christian truth, God's only agent on earth. Yet both empires were flawed. In the east, Islam threatened a direct assault, heresies and sects nibbled at the Truth, barbarians assailed its flanks. In the west, Charlemagne, the Frankish king, had had himself crowned emperor in AD 800, founding a new Roman empire – but an empire divided against itself, with royal heirs and a pope all rivalling each other. Greek was for the east, Latin for the west. Political and social differences focused on a doctrinal dispute about the nature of the godhead which would in the end prove irresolvable. Both dreamed of a united Christendom, but by 800 the two empires were breaking apart like two drifting continental plates.

On their borders, their grinding division left fault lines, in particular in the pagan region to the north of Byzantium, and to the east of Charlemagne's empire, from today's Balkans up through present-day Russia. This vast area seethed with migrants pouring in from the east and north, Turks and Slavs in numerous tribes – Avars, Bulgars, Pechenegs, Khazars – and then Scandinavians striking south along the river roads from the Baltic. Rome and Byzantium both turned to these benighted regions to secure their borderlands. Roman missionaries penetrated north and east, into Bohemia. Missionaries from Byzantium moved through Greece, into Slav lands. The result was a patchwork of tribes and kingdoms, all jockeying to increase wealth and influence – which for all of them meant an accommodation with one or other of the forms of Christianity – all reacting in unpredictable ways to the meddling of the two super-powers. Eastern

Europe had scarcely begun to settle – the Hungarians had not even appeared on the eastern horizon yet – but the fault lines created as the two empires ground out their destinies are visible today, in the scripts that still divide them.

One main Slav region had become a kingdom by the early ninth century – Moravia, in the south-east of today's Czech Republic. Moravia, which takes its name from the Morava river running between the present-day Czech Republic and Slovakia into the Danube, was strategically important, dominating the river route from German lands to the Black Sea. Through Moravia flowed silk, ivory, spices and incense that found their way to northern monasteries, and Moravian chiefs became rich in jewellery, pottery and swords, as their excavated graves reveal. The heirs of Charlemagne, pushing eastwards, could not afford to ignore Moravia; and vice versa.

Downriver was Bulgaria, where Slavs had forced their way in among long-established Turks. By the ninth century, they ruled from the Black Sea to the Carpathians and southwards to the borders of Greece. An attempt by Byzantium to impose its will on Bulgaria had ended badly, when the emperor Nicephorus died in combat, his skull being encased in silver by his enemy and turned into a drinking goblet. Meanwhile, Byzantium, having dammed the rising tide of Islam, turned its gaze, and the attention of its missionaries, back to the Balkans. The Bulgarians were to Byzantium what the Moravians were to Charlemagne's Holy Roman Empire.

In mid-century, both Moravia and Bulgaria had kings, Rastislav in Moravia and Boris in Bulgaria. Both faced an eternal conundrum. To acquire wealth demanded trade; trade demanded a relationship with larger powers; but a relationship threatened independence. Both feared and courted their respective imperial neighbours. In Moravia, Rastislav was wary of western imperialism, in the form of two rival missionary drives, from Germany and Italy. Boris was equally wary of neighbouring Byzantium.

Boris gave the increasing spiral of tension a crucial twist in 862. Nervous of Rastislav's growing power, and seeking to escape the tentacles of Byzantium, he met Charlemagne's grandson, Louis the German, king of Bavaria. Louis, of course, had his own agenda, which did not include his nominal overlords, the emperor and the pope. Rastislav foresaw danger – Germans to the left, Germans to the right, and Moravia swallowed. His response was to send an embassy to Michael III in Constantinople with an urgent request: for a 'teacher to instruct us in the true faith in our own language'.

The request came at a crucial moment for Michael. Two years earlier, the Russians had struck. Actually, they were Vikings, transplanted to Kiev on the Dnieper, and now known as 'Rus'. Although they had started trading along the 'river roads' with the newly established empire of Islam, to the Byzantines the two hundred-strong fleet appeared out of nowhere. Michael suddenly had a new enemy north of the Black Sea, dangerously close to a Byzantine colony in the Crimea. And now the Bulgarians were in talks with a German king, surely a vanguard of Rome. Michael could do with an ally north of the Bosphorus. Rastislav's embassy must have seemed a godsend, literally.

Michael had one small problem with the Moravian request. There were only three languages suitable for the administration of the sacraments: Latin, Greek and Hebrew, the languages in which Pilate had ordered the notice placed above Christ on the cross. But this was no time for niceties. Michael ordered a mission that would serve both his own interests and Rastislav's, preaching in Slavonic.

The mission was to be headed by two brothers, Methodius, then about forty-seven, and Constantine, the younger by twelve years. They were uniquely qualified for the task. Constantine, nicknamed 'the Philosopher', was one of the greatest scholars of the day, and Methodius had been governor of a Slavonic province. Both had already headed a mission to the Turkic-speaking Khazars (too late as it happened: the Khazars had already opted for Judaism). And both had been raised in Thessalonica, a frontier town between Byzantium and Slavic southern Macedonia. In its streets, Slavonic and Greek were spoken side by side. The brothers were bilingual.

Before leaving Byzantium, Constantine tackled the problem of teaching Christianity in Slavonic. To this end, he invented a new alphabet, which came to be called Glagolitic, from the Slavonic root for 'word' and 'to speak'. Possibly, the name was inspired by the frequent 'he said' (*glagola*) in the Slavonic liturgy, or by one of the first passages he translated into Slavonic, the opening of St John's Gospel: 'In the beginning was the word.' If the Glagolitic alphabet was all Constantine's own work, it was an astounding intellectual achievement, because it apparently fitted old Slavonic superbly. But many doubt that he was the sole inventor. His brother was probably involved, as were the many Slavic-speaking monks who were to accompany them to Moravia. In any event, the probable inspiration was a written form of Greek, which Constantine, either on his own or at the head of a committee, brilliantly modified into forty new letters. Though soon superseded in most Slavic-speaking areas, Glagolitic remained as a crumbling bastion against Roman influence in Croatia until the early nineteenth century.

The language fixed by the new alphabet, known as Old Church Slavonic, was then understood by all Slav speakers, whether they lived in present-day Serbia, Croatia, Bulgaria or Russia. It was in this language, in Constantine's translation, that the Gospels appeared – the first Bible translation in a vernacular language in the west. You can still hear it today in the services of the Russian Orthodox Church.

For a few years, the mission teetered between success

and failure. Pope Hadrian II backed the brothers, because their influence counteracted the ambitions of his nominal subjects, the Germans. On a visit to Rome in 868, Constantine and Methodius were honoured with liturgies in Slavonic. But Constantine fell ill. While on his deathbed, he expressed the wish to die as a monk. According to Byzantine custom, he took a new name with the same initial letter, and died a month later re-christened Cyril, aged only fifty-two. Methodius, named a papal legate, was to continue the good work back in Moravia, but by the time he arrived, Rastislav had been ousted by a pro-German faction. German clergy in Moravia were incensed: they had been working in Latin to convert Slavs for seventy-five years, and here was a jumped-up Greek aiming to introduce *Greek* services in *Slavonic*! Methodius was arrested on trumped-up charges and kept in prison secretly for almost three years, until the Pope heard of it and ordered his release. When he returned, the German clergy were in full control. After he died in 885, his team of clergy were expelled.

That was the ignominious end of the Orthodoxy in Moravia; and that is why Czechs and Slovaks today look to the west, and use the Latin alphabet.

Meanwhile, to turn back the clock almost twenty years, Michael III, galvanized by Boris's rapprochement with

Louis the German, had sent an army and a navy to retrieve Bulgaria. The Pope turned a deaf ear to Boris's plea for help. Boris had little option. In 864, he became Michael's godson, allowed himself to be baptised, expelled Latin clergy, and invited in Byzantine priests. For fifteen years, his mixed Turkish–Slav population resisted the influence of their traditional enemies, the Greeks. Then the expulsion of Methodius's clergy from Moravia injected new life into Bulgarian Orthodoxy. Moravian priests brought with them expertise in Old Church Slavonic and the Glagolitic alphabet. A new school system trained some 3500 disciples who were sent off around the country. Boris's son and heir, Simeon, built a new residency at Preslav, soon to become the greatest of Balkan cities, with several monasteries and a twelve-apsed 'Golden Church', the ruins of which now host only a few tourists.

It seems that Bulgarians found the Glagolitic alphabet, rooted in a cursive form of Greek, hard going. But Bulgarian scholars were familiar with Greek *capital* letters (uncials), and around AD 893 came up with a revised alphabet they named after the father of Slavic Christianity, formerly Constantine, now St Cyril. Though Cyrillic honours Cyril's memory, it was not invented by him, as countless books claim. His own invention slowly faded in competition with the one that bears his name.

Thus Bulgaria became the first Slav national church, a

bastion both of Orthodoxy and Cyrillic. Its new alphabet allowed it to develop its own literature, and buttressed a doomed bid for independence, which finally ended in a truly horrible fashion in 1014, when the Byzantine emperor, Basil, 'the Bulgarian slayer', put out the eyes of 14,000 captive Bulgarians. By then, its religion and its script had been an inspiration for another barbarian culture emerging 600 miles to the north.

In origin, St Vladimir, king of Kievan Russia, was anything but a saint. Part-Viking, part-Slav, Volodimir (as he is in another spelling) was an enthusiast for ancient Slavonic gods. He came to the throne by killing his brother. He had four wives and (it was said) eight hundred concubines, a fair figure, perhaps, given that he reputedly gave vent to a ferocious sexual drive in every town and village he visited. On his succession in 980, he put up statues to his pagan gods in Kiev, and celebrated by sacrificing a thousand victims in public.

Vladimir was in a position to see that such acts would do him little good in the long run. Kiev was the centre of that 'water road' of rivers, principally the Dnieper, linking Scandinavia and Byzantium. Men of many religions gathered there: Christians, Muslims, even some Jews. Eastwards lay pagan nomads, south and west were Christian kings in rich cities. To an ambitious leader, it must have been clear that monotheism spelled civilization, stability and wealth, while paganism, reviled by literate and rich foreign traders, would lead to war, with the attendant risk of defeat and poverty.

The Russian Primary Chronicle, edited by a Kievan monk, Nestor, in about 1100, tells a famous story. In 987, Vladimir decided he needed a new religion. But which? He sent out a team of researchers. When they returned, he went through the options. The Jews were scattered, and powerless, so Judaism was out. Islam was discarded when Vladimir learned they were against alcohol; for Russians, he said, happiness was quite impossible without strong drink. The Catholics looked to the Pope, and one thing Vladimir did not need was the challenge of another strong leader. In Germany, complained his envoys, 'we saw no beauty'.

But in Constantinople lay perfection. His delegates reported that in the great church of St Sophia a ceremony was put on for them. Its awe-inspiring theatricality – gorgeous costumes, imposing priests, incense-laden air, music to seize the soul – staggered them. Their words to Vladimir have often been quoted: 'We knew not whether we were in heaven or on earth, for on earth there is no such vision or beauty, and we do not know how to describe it; we only know that there God dwells among men.'

It is a good tale, which conceals as much as it tells. Vladimir's grandmother, Olga, had been baptized in Constantinople in about 957. As regent of Kievan Russia,

Olga, the first Russian saint, was one of the most formidable ladies of her age. In the words of Nestor's chronicle, she 'was radiant among the infidels like a pearl in the mire'. With her as an example, Vladimir must have had a fair idea of the benefits of Orthodoxy, without inquiring too deeply into alternatives.

There were other complexities. Vladimir did not simply convert, inviting in a foreign culture that might threaten his independence. It was a decision taken as part of a portfolio of military, political and cultural considerations. His father, Svyatoslav, once held captive in Constantinople, had gained his freedom by promising to send help if needed. When Basil II, the 'Slayer of the Bulgarians', needed to crush a revolt, Vladimir sent six thousand soldiers as part of a deal: Vladimir to become a Christian, Basil to hand over his sister Anna in marriage.

In Kiev, Orthodox priests set about the job of converting Rus to the new religion, using Cyrillic to lever Vladimir's Slavic population into the modern world of literacy and Christianity. Perun, the old god of gods, with his silver head and golden moustaches, was toppled from his hilltop shrine above Kiev and rolled into the Dnieper. In the 1050s, Hilarion, the first Russian Metropolitan, recalled those days: 'Angel's trumpet and God's thunder sounded through all the towns. The air was sanctified by the incense that ascended towards God. Monasteries stood on the mountain.' Vladimir turned from womanizing to converting, acting as godfather to hundreds, opening schools, setting up courts and building innumerable churches and monasteries, including Kiev's great Cathedral for the Tithes. He died in 1015 and in due course was made a saint.

The consequences of Vladimir's action transformed Russian culture. Russian churches, with their central and subsidiary domes, were Byzantine. Kiev, with its own St Sophia, became 'the glory of Greece'. Byzantine law became the basis of Russian law. Missionaries spread both script and scriptures. Cyrillic remained the basis of Russian literature (and that of other Orthodox Slav cultures: Belorussian, Serbian, Bulgarian, Macedonian, Ukrainian). When the tattered remnants of Byzantium fell to the Turks in 1453, it was the Russian church that became the champion of Orthodoxy. 'There exists only one true church on earth,' wrote the Metropolitan, the Russian Orthodox leader. 'The Church of Russia.'

The two systems staked their claims, the Roman alphabet in western Europe, Cyrillic to the east. Each proved as adaptable as the other, ballooning outwards in the eighteenth- and nineteenth-century drive to empire.

As Russia pursued her manifest destiny east across Siberia and south into the Caucasus and Central Asia, her soldiers, administrators, missionaries and scientists carried Cyrillic with them. In large measure, the advance was a long-term assault on Islam, an assault that increased in intensity with every increase in control from Moscow. After fifty years, it came to a head in the 1930s under Josef Stalin, whose determination to seize economic power and destroy traditional beliefs and power-structures was genocidal. In Kazakhstan alone, a population of four million in 1926 had been reduced to three million by the time of the 1939 census. With war on the horizon, Stalin demanded unity, by which he meant total obedience. In 1939, Cyrillic was imposed on all the language groups of Central Asia – though this was not a fate Stalin imposed on his own people, the Georgians, whose alphabet, *mxedruli*, still thrives. For others, Muslims in particular, it was a sort of cultural blinding. Muslim peoples in Soviet Central Asia were cut off from their histories, their literatures and the wider Islamic world. At a stroke, they were rendered illiterate and politically impotent. In the terms stated by George Orwell in *1984*, they became un-people. The policy was relaxed somewhat under Stalin's successors, but all Central Asia continued to write in Cyrillic, which is now used to write some fifty languages. There was no forced conversion in the long-established cultures of the post-war Soviet empire in eastern Europe, and the borders were mildly elastic – Rumanian switched from Cyrillic to Roman in the nineteenth century, in deference to its Romance ancestry, and never switched back.

Further east still, in Mongolia, a script was still in use some 600 years after its first introduction on the orders of

Chingis Khan. Though the ways of its semi-nomadic herd-
ers would have been instantly recognizable to Chingis,
Mongolia was a unique political creation. It was the second
socialist nation, having become independent of China and
then Communist, under Soviet aegis, in 1924. Though a
Marxist state, it lacked industry, and thus a working-class
proletariat. To Marxists, it was an affront. So was its
graceful vertical script, which was not only a symbol of its
feudal background, but was a living fossil. When reading it
today (for it is still in use in Inner Mongolia), it is something like reading Chaucer, but pronouncing his words as
modern English. By 1940, the pressures for change had
become overwhelming. Stalin had a Mongolian counterpart in the poisonous Choibalsan, who had overseen the
destruction of 1000 monasteries. Soviet troops had just
stood shoulder-to-shoulder with Mongols to block Japanese expansion into Mongolia and the Soviet Far East. A
change of script was just the thing to assert Mongolia's
separation from Japanese and Chinese hegemony, and its
new affiliation. In 1941, the Party opted for Cyrillic, which
was introduced the following year. Oppression and practicality were both served, for the revised script fitted the
language far better than the old. By 1990, it was a rarity for
people under forty to read the vertical script. After the
rejection of Communism in 1990–2, there was a move to
reinstate it but its time had passed. There was no stomach,
or cash, to turn back the clock. Despite a somewhat
schizophrenic attitude towards things Russian, the Russian

script – in essence the one devised by Greek monks for Slav-speakers a thousand years before – is in Mongolia to stay.

The Roman alphabet, having coped with Hungarian, Finnish and Basque, proved equally handy outside Europe. Mainly as the result of missionary activity, some five hundred African languages have now been recorded in the Roman script. Secure, conservative cultures easily preserved their scripts. In India, two centuries of British rule brought in a new language and script alongside the old ones. French scholars converted Vietnamese into Roman, in large measure because that helped the Vietnamese separate from their big brother, China. (Cambodia, with its ancient and long-established Khmer script, was well protected against such meddling.) Spain carried the Roman script to the Philippines, Holland took it to Indonesia, Spain and Portugal to South America (consigning Mayan hieroglyphs to oblivion until they were resurrected over the last few decades).

The drive to Romanize continues to this day. In Dallas missionary-linguists of the Summer Institute of Linguistics (or the Wesley Bible Translators: which title is used depends on context) still reduce unrecorded languages to writing. Their aim is to translate the Bible into every surviving language, an odd ambition that has produced highly controversial results in anthropological terms but also some extraordinarily fine work in linguistics, which never uses anything but Roman orthography. The 600-

strong tribe with which I worked, the Waorani of eastern Ecuador, read their language (or some of them do) in the letters brought by American missionaries; and when the language dies, as it surely will, Waorani descendants will read in the language and letters of the Spanish-speaking culture of a nation to which they did not know they belonged until the 1960s.

There is one fast-evolving culture still working out its own answers to the use of script: the Internet. Like it or not, computers and the Internet are western inventions. The technology is western based, the terminology is western, the keyboards are mostly in the alphabet that would be familiar to a Roman of 2400 years ago. Arabic- and Cyrillic-using countries have long had a tradition of studying western European languages, principally English, so the Latin alphabet is familiar enough to almost anyone with a higher education. For a few years, as the Internet became established, the technology favoured those who could communicate using the ABC. The base-code ASCII was the *American* Standard Code for Information Interchange. In the mid-1990s, anyone who risked a prediction might have said that the Roman alphabet would soon rule in cyberspace.

Not any more. Any script – like Arabic, for example – can be protected by dual keyboards which can be switched back and forth between the local and Roman scripts. Standard programs can import an Arabic document as a picture (if you can bear to wait for it to download). And a new standard seems almost certain to become universal, the Unicode, which stores all characters of 143 (and rising) scripts, including Chinese, independent of program and language. For pc users, language will remain a barrier to be crossed by translation, and keyboards will need to be customized, but on the Internet scripts will all be fully convertible.

In China, though, the future for the Roman alphabet looks rosy – but without displacing traditional Chinese script. Anyone using a pc in China must be Roman-literate to use a keyboard. E-mails, still used by the literate few who communicate abroad, are often written in English anyway. Working in Chinese, you type using the Roman system: Pinyin. Since Pinyin does not indicate the *tones* of Chinese, the program displays a selection of characters that suit the context and you choose the appropriate one. It is a cumbersome system, which may be superseded by the next generation of computers, in which voice-recognition may do away with the need to type at all.

There are a number of forces at work here. Pinyin, not much used within China, might even alienate potential customers. On the other hand it is vital for contact with the west and for the acquisition of new technology. It is also a handy way for a central government to impose

Mandarin Chinese on its diverse peoples. Certainly, for westerners, Pinyin is a great way of communicating with Chinese.

By an odd irony, it seems that the most conservative and most ancient of writing systems can only sustain itself by going into partnership with its upstart rival from Rome.

APPENDIX 1

A family tree tracing the origins of our alphabet appears overleaf.

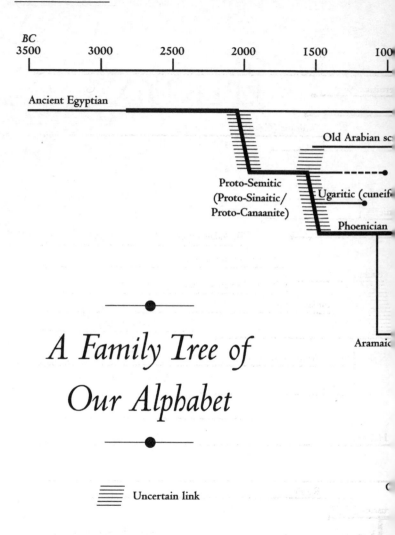

A Family Tree of Our Alphabet

Uncertain link

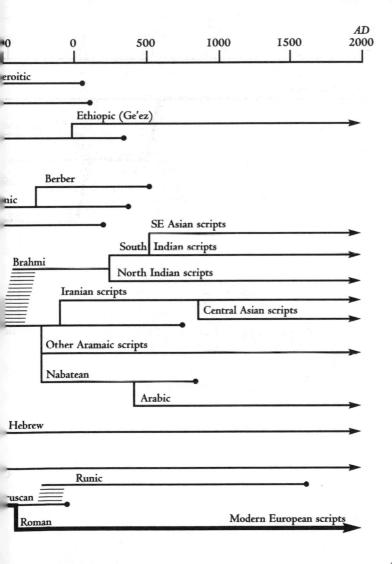

APPENDIX 2

The following pages show some major alphabets and their widely accepted transliterations.

Hieroglyphic alphabet

phonological value	conventional transliteration	sign	entity represented
a glottal stop (as in Cockney 'bottle')	ꜣ	𓄿	Egyptian vulture
y (as in 'yoke')	j	𓇋	reed
y	jj, y	𓏭 (or *n*)	two reeds
a gutteral sound (Arabic *ayin*)	ꜥ	𓂝	forearm
w	w	𓅱 (or 𓏲)	quail chick
b	b	𓃀	foot
p	p	𓊪	stool(?)
f	f	𓆑	horned viper
m	m	𓅓 (or 𓐝 or 𓌳)	owl
n	n	𓈖 (or 𓋔)	water
r	r	𓂋	mouth
h (as in 'he')	h	𓉔	reed shelter
emphatic h	ḥ	𓎛	twisted wick
ch (as in German 'Buch')	ḫ	𓐍	placenta(?)
ch (as in German 'ich')	ẖ	𓄡	animal's belly
z	z	𓊃	door-bolt
s	s	𓋴	folded cloth
sh (as in 'she')	š	𓈙	pool
q (as in 'queen')	q (or ḳ)	𓈎	hill-slope
k	k	𓎡	basket
hard g	g	𓎼	jar-stand
t	t	𓏏	loaf of bread
ch (as in 'choke')	ṯ	𓍿	rope tether
d	d	𓂧	hand
j (as in 'joke')	ḏ	𓆓	snake

(from Richard Parkinson, *Cracking Codes*)

Proto-Sinaitic and Ugaritic alphabets

sign (with variants)	transliteration
𓃾	*3* glottal stop
⬠ ☐	*b*
∟	*g* (?)
⬡	*d*
Ψ Ⴘ	*h*
♀	*w*
=	*ḏ*
⧉ ⬚ 𐤇 𐤇	*ḥ*
∟ ～	*y*
Ш	*k*
⌐℘ᛋ	*l*
∿∿ ～～	*m*
～～～ ～ ∟	*n*
⬭ ◊	*'* gutteral
⌣	*p*
Ⅴ Ⴤ	*ṣ*
𐌏	*q*
𐌒 𐌐 𐌓	*r*
ω Ⴤ	*š*
+ ✕	*t*
⊥⚬ Ψ ♡ 𐌇	signs with unknown value

(from Benjamin Sass, The Genesis of the Alphabet and Its Development in the 2nd Millennium)

Ugaritic	Transliteration
⤚	ʾa
𐎁	b
𐎂	g
𐎃	ḫ
𐎄	d
𐎅	h
𐎆	w
𐎇	z
𐎈	ḥ
𐎉	ṭ
𐎊	y
𐎋	k
𐎌	š
𐎍	l
𐎎	m
𐎏	ḏ
𐎐	n
𐎑	ẓ
𐎒	s
𐎓	ʿ
𐎔	p
𐎕	ṣ
𐎖	q
𐎗	r
𐎘	t
𐎙	ġ
𐎚	t
𐎛	ʾi
𐎜	ʾu
𐎝	s̀

Phoenician and Hebrew alphabets

Letter name	Phonetic value	Phoenician	Modern Hebrew
'Āleph	'A	∢	א
Bēth	B	⅊	ב
Gimel	G	⅂	ג
Dāleth	D	△	ד
Hē	H	⅄	ה
Wāw	V	Y	ו
Zayin	Z	⏖	ז
Ḥēth	CH	⊟	ח
Ṭēth	T	⊗	ט
Yōdh	Y	⊿	י
Kaph	K	⅄	כ
Lāmadh	L	⫇	ל
Mēm	M	ⱳ	מ
Nūn	N	ⱴ	נ
Sāmekh	S	⸓	ס
'Ayin	A	ο	ע
Pē	P	⅂	פ
Ṣādē	TS	⌐	צ
Qōph	Q	Φ	ק
Rēš	R	◁	ר
Šīn	SH	W	ש
Tāw	T	✕	ת

Greek alphabet

Name	800 - 600 BC	Upper Case	Lower Case	Transliteration
alpha	AΛΛ	A	α	a
bēta	ℇ Ɓ B	B	β	b
gamma	Γ Γ C	Γ	γ	g
delta	▷ △ D	Δ	δ	d
e psilon	⋿ Ⅎ E	E	ε	e
digamma	F F ⊏			
zēta	I ⵣ I	Z	ζ	z
ēta	⊟ ⴙ H	H	η	e, ē
thēta	⊗ ⊕ ⊙	Θ	θ	th
iōta	⟨ ⸹ I	I	ι	i
kappa	K K K	K	κ	k
lambda	L Γ Λ	Λ	λ	l
mu	⋎ ⋏M	M	μ	m
nu	Γ Γ N	N	ν	n
ksi	丰 王 ≡	Ξ	ξ	x
o mikron	O	O	o	o
pi	Γ Γ	Π	π	p
san	M			
qoppa	Φ Ϙ			
rhō	P D ꓤ	P	ρ	r
sigma	⟨ ⸹ ⸹	Σ	π,ς¹	s
tau	T	T	τ	t
u psilon	Γ Y V	Y	υ	y
phi	Φ ⊕ ⚭	Φ	φ	ph
chi	X ✛	X	χ	ch, kh
psi	Y ⋎	Ψ	ψ	ps
ō mega	⋂ Ω Ω	Ω	ω	o, ō

Etruscan alphabet

	Etruscan	Early Latin
a	𐌀	𐌀
b	𐌁	
c/g	𐌂	𐌂
d	𐌃	𐌃
e	𐌄	𐌄
v	𐌅	
z [ts]	𐌆	
h	𐌇	𐌇
th	𐌈	
i	𐌉	𐌉
k	𐌊	𐌊
l	𐌋	𐌋
m	𐌌	𐌌
n	𐌍	𐌍
š	𐌎	
o	𐌏	𐌏
p	𐌐	𐌐
ś	𐌑	
q	𐌒	𐌒
r	𐌓	𐌓
s	𐌔	𐌔
t	𐌕	𐌕
u	𐌖	𐌖
ś, x	𐌗	𐌗
ph	𐌘	
ch	𐌙	
f		𐌚

Slavic alphabets

OCS Gyrillic	Glagolitic OCS	Modern Russian	Transliteration
а	ⰰ	А	a
б	ⰱ	Б	b
в	ⰲ	В	v
г	ⰳ	Г	g
д	ⰴ	Д	d
є	ⰵ	Е (Ё)	e / i͡o
ж	ⰶ	Ж	zh
ѕ	ⰷ		ż
з	ⰸ	З	z
и	ⰹ	И	i
ї/ı	ⰺ/ⰻ	Й	ī
ћ	ⰼ		ǵ
к	ⰽ	К	k
л	ⰾ	Л	l
м	ⰿ	М	m
н	ⱀ	Н	n
о	ⱁ	О	o
п	ⱂ	П	p
р	ⱃ	Р	r
с	ⱄ	С	s
т	ⱅ	Т	t
оу/ȣ	ⱆ	У	u/ū
ф	ⱇ	Ф	f
х	ⱈ	Х	kh
ω/ѽ	ⱉ		ō
ц	ⱌ	Ц	t͡s
ч	ⱍ	Ч	ch
ш	ⱎ	Ш	sh
ш	ⱋ		sht
		Щ	shch
ъ	ⱏ/ⱐ	Ъ	[hard sign]
ы/ъи	ⱏⰹ ⱏⰺ/ⱐⰹ ⱐⰺ	Ы	y
ь	ⱐ	Ь	[soft sign]
		Э	ė
ѣ	ⱑ		ě
ю	ⱓ	Ю	i͡u
ꙗ		Я	i͡a
ѥ			i͡e
ѧ	ⱔ		ę
ѩ	ⱗ		i͡ę
ѫ	ⱘ		ǫ
ѭ	ⱙ		i͡ǫ
ѯ			k͡s
ѱ			p͡s
ѡ	ⱚ		t̄
ѵ	ⱛ		v̇

Korean alphabet

Hankul	Yale transliteration	Hankul	Yale transliteration
ㄱ	k	오	o
ㄲ	kk	요	yo
ㄴ	n	와	wa
ㄷ	t	왜	way
ㄸ	tt	외	oy
ㄹ	l	우	wu
ㅁ	m	워	we
ㅂ	p	웨	wey
ㅃ	pp	위	wi
ㅅ	s	유	yu
ㅆ	ss	으	u
ㅇ	-ng	의	uy
아	a	이	i
애	ay	ㅈ	c
야	ya	ㅉ	cc
애	yay	ㅊ	ch
어	e	ㅋ	kh
에	ey	ㅌ	th
여	ye	ㅍ	ph
예	yey	ㅎ	h

BIBLIOGRAPHY

General

Daniels, P. T., and Bright, W. (eds.), *The World's Writing Systems*, New York and Oxford, 1996.

DeFrancis, John, *Visible Speech: The Diverse Oneness of Writing Systems*, Honolulu, 1989.

Diringer, David, *The Alphabet: A Key to the History of Mankind* (2 vols.), London, 1968.

Cambridge Ancient History, Vol II, Middle East and Aegean: part 1 (1800–1380) and *Part 2 (1380–1000)*.

Gelb, I. J., *A Study of Writing*, Chicago, 1952, 1963.

Goody, Jack, *The Interface Between the Written and the Oral*, Cambridge, 1987.

Havelock, Eric, *The Muse Learns to Write*, New Haven, London, 1986.

Healey, John, *The Early Alphabet*, London, 1990.

Jean, Georges, *Writing: The Story of Alphabets and Scripts*, London, 1992.

Lord, Albert B., *The Singer of Tales*, Harvard, Oxford, 1960.

Pope, Maurice, *The Story of Decipherment*, London, 1999.

Shlain, Leonard, *The Alphabet Versus the Goddess*, New York, 1998/London, 1999.

The Ancient Eastern Mediterranean

George, Andrew, *The Epic of Gilgamesh: A New Translation*, London, 1999.

Godart, Louis, *The Phaistos Disc: The Enigma of an Aegean Script*, Iraklion, 1995.

Gordon, Cyrus, *Forgotten Scripts: The Story of their Decipherment*, London, 1971.

James, Peter, *Centuries of Darkness*, London, 1991.

Parkinson, Richard, *The Tale of Sinuhe and Other Ancient Egyptian Poems, 1940–1640 BC*, Oxford, 1998; *Cracking Codes: The Rosetta Stone and Decipherment*, London, 1999.

Walker, C. B. F., *Cuneiform*, London, 1987, 1988.

Canaan

Albright, William Foxwell, 'The Role of the Canaanites in the History of Civilization' in *The Bible and the Ancient Near East: Essays in honour of William Foxwell Albright*, London, 1961.

Armstrong, Karen, *The History of God*, London, 1993.

Bernstein, Burton, *Sinai, The Great and Terrible Wilderness*, London, 1979.

Briquel-Chatonnet, Françoise, 'Les Inscriptions Protosinaïtiques' in Dominique Valbelle and Charles Bonnet (eds.), *Le Sinaï Durant L'Antiquité et Le Moyen Âge*, Paris, 1998.

Drower, Margaret S. *Flinders Petrie: A Life in Archaeology*, Wisconsin, London, 1985/1995.

Frerichs, Ernest S. and Leonard Lesko (eds.), *Exodus: The Egyptian Evidence*, Winona Lake, 1997.

Gardiner, Alan, 'The Egyptian Origin of the Semitic Alphabet' in *The Journal of Egyptian Archaeology, III*, London, 1916.

Gordon, Cyrus, *Before the Bible*, London, 1962.

Naveh, Joseph, *Early History of the Alphabet*, Brill, 1982.

Niditch, Susan, *Oral World and Written Word: Orality and Literacy in Ancient Israel*, Kentucky, 1996/London, 1997.

Petrie, W. M. Flinders, *Researches in Sinai*, London, 1906.

Sass, Benjamin, *The Genesis of the Alphabet and Its Development in the 2nd Millennium*, Wiesbaden, 1988; *Studia Alphabetica: On the Origin and early History of the Northwest Semitic, South Semitic and Greek Alphabets*, Göttingen, 1991.

Phoenicia

Craigie, Peter, *Ugaritic and the Old Testament*, Grand Rapids, 1983.

Markoe, Glenn E., *Phoenicians*, London, 2000.

Pritchard, James, *The Ancient Near East: An Anthology of Texts and Pictures*, Princeton, Oxford, 1958.

Watson, Wilfred and Nicolas Wyatt (eds), *Handbook of Ugaritic Studies*, Brill, 1999.

Wyatt, Nicolas (ed.), *Religious Texts from Ugarit*, Sheffield, 1998.

Greece

American School of Classical Studies at Athens, *Graffiti in the Athenian Agora*, New Jersey, 1974.

Bernal, Martin, *Cadmean Letters*, Winona Lake, 1990.

Calasso, Roberto, *The Marriage of Cadmus and Harmony*, Milan, 1998/New York, London, 1993.

Havelock, Eric, *The Literate Revolution in Greece and Its Cultural Consequences*, New Jersey, 1982; *Preface to Plato*, Oxford, 1963.

MacLeod, Roy (ed.), *The Library of Alexandria*, London, New York, 2000.

Morris, Ian and Barry Powell, *A New Companion to Homer*, Brill, 1997.

Powell, Barry, *Homer and the Origin of the Greek Alphabet*, Cambridge, 1991.

Ridgway, David, *The First Western Greeks*, Cambridge, 1992.

Taplin, Oliver, *Greek Fire*, London, 1989.

West, M. L., *The East Face of Helicon: West Asiatic Elements in Greek Poetry and Myth*, Oxford, 1997.

Williamson, Margaret, *Sappho's Immortal Daughters*, Cambridge, Mass., 1995.

Woodard, Roger, *Greek Writing from Knossos to Homer*, New York, Oxford, 1997.

Etruscan/Roman

Banti, Luisa, *Etruscan Cities and Their Culture*, London, 1973.

Barker, Graeme and Tom Rasmussen, *The Etruscans*, Oxford and Malden, Mass., 1998.

Grant, Michael, *The Etruscans*, London, 1980.

Keller, Werner, *The Etruscans*, New York, 1974.

Welford, James, *The Search for the Etruscans*, London, 1973.

Linguistics

Blackmore, Susan, *The Meme Machine*, Oxford, 1999.

Collins, Beverley, and Inger Mees, *The Real Professor Higgins: The Life and Career of Daniel Jones*, Berlin, 1999.

Kim-Renaud, Young-Key (ed.), *The Korean Alphabet*, Honolulu, 1997; *King Sejong the Great*, Washington, 1997.

Cyrillic

Dvornik, Francis, *Byzantine Missions Among the Slavs*, Boston, Mass., 1970.

Obolensky, Dimitri, *Byzantium and the Slavs*, New York, 1994.

ACKNOWLEDGEMENTS

The prime mover in this project was Doug Young at Hodder-Headline: to an exemplary editor and exemplary publishers, my thanks.

My thanks also to the following for their forbearance, and the generosity with which they shared their expertise: David Bennett, Senior Lecturer in Linguistics, School of Oriental and African Studies, London; Susan Blackmore, Dept. of Psychology, Faculty of Applied Science, University of the West of England, Bristol; Tony Cheng, BBC World Service (Chinese); John Darnell, Senior Epigrapher at the Epigraphic Survey, Luxor, and Research Associate, Oriental Institute, University of Chicago; Deborah Darnell, Epigrapher and Librarian, Epigraphic Survey, Luxor; Martina Deuchler, Professor of Korean Studies, School of Oriental and African Studies, London; Trevor Ford and Marianne Barton; Andrew George, Reader in Assyriology, School of Oriental and

African Studies, London; Christopher Gill, Professor of Classics, Exeter University; Khin-Wai-Thi, UNESCO, Geneva; Terence Mitchell, Western Asiatic Antiquities, British Museum; Michael MacMahon, Department of English Language, University of Glasgow; Joe Mulrooney, Lecturer in Biblical Studies, Heythrop College, University of London; Iain Murray, Department of Applied Computing, University of Dundee; Richard Parkinson, Department of Egyptian Antiquities, British Museum; Professor Paul Richardson, School of Art Publishing and Music, Oxford Brookes University; Benjamin Sass, Department of Archaeology, University of Haifa; Thomas Sebeok, Emeritus Professor of Linguistics and Semiotics, Indiana University; Greg Stevenson, International Federation of the Periodical Press; Judith Swaddling, Department of Greek and Roman Antiquities, British Museum; Oliver Taplin, Professor of Classics, Magdalen College, Oxford; Wilfred Watson, Department of Religious Studies, Newcastle University; John Wells, Professor of Phonetics, University College, London; Margaret Williamson, Associate Professor of Classics and Comparative Literature, Dartmouth College, Hanover, New Hampshire.

INDEX

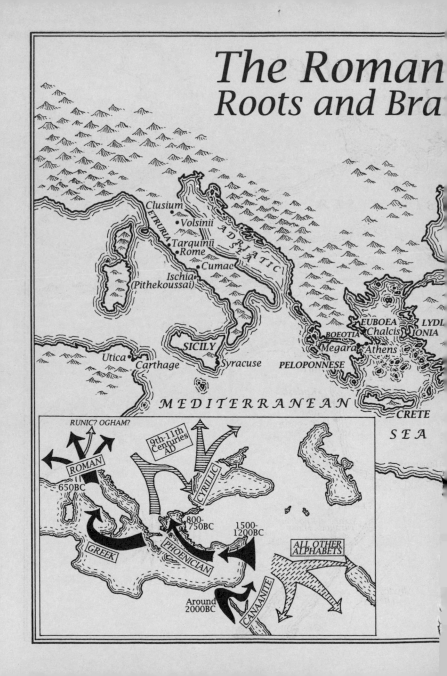